Young People's Transitions into Creative Work

Exploring how formal and informal education initiatives and training systems in the US, UK, and Australia seek to achieve a socially diverse workforce, this insightful book offers a series of detailed case studies to reveal the initiative and ingenuity shown by today's young people as they navigate entry into creative fields of work.

Young People's Transitions into Creative Work acknowledges the new and diverse challenges faced by today's youth as they look to enter employment. Chapters trace the rise of indie work, aspirational labour, economic precarity, and disruptive effects of digital technologies to illustrate the inventive ways in which youth from varied socioeconomic and cultural backgrounds enter into work in film, games production, music, and visual arts. From hip-hop to new media arts, the text explores how opportunities for creative work have multiplied in recent years as digital technologies open new markets, new scenes, and new opportunities for entrepreneurs and innovation.

This book will be of great interest to researchers, academics, and postgraduate students in the fields of youth studies, careers guidance, media studies, vocational education, and sociology of education.

Julian Sefton-Green is Professor of New Media Education at Deakin University, Australia.

S. Craig Watkins is Founding Director of the Institute for Media Innovation and the incoming Ernest S. Sharpe Centennial Professor in the Moody College of Communication at the University of Texas at Austin, USA.

Ben Kirshner is Professor of Education at the University of Colorado Boulder and Faculty Director of CU Engage: Center for Community-Based Learning and Research, USA.

Routledge Research in Education

This series aims to present the latest research from right across the field of education. It is not confined to any particular area or school of thought and seeks to provide coverage of a broad range of topics, theories and issues from around the world.

Recent titles in the series include:

For a complete list of titles in this series, please visit: www.routledge.com/Routledge-Research-in-Education/book-series/SE0393

Young People's Transitions into Creative Work

Navigating Challenges and Opportunities

Julian Sefton-Green, S. Craig Watkins
and Ben Kirshner

Routledge
Taylor & Francis Group

LONDON AND NEW YORK

First published 2020 by Routledge

2 Park Square, Milton Park, Abingdon, Oxon, OX14 4RN

605 Third Avenue, New York, NY 10017

Routledge is an imprint of the Taylor & Francis Group, an informa business

First issued in paperback 2020

Library of Congress Cataloging-in-Publication Data
A catalog record for this book has been requested

ISBN: 978-1-138-04083-0 (hbk)
ISBN: 978-0-367-77743-2 (pbk)

Typeset in Sabon
by Apex CoVantage, LLC

Contents

Figures and Table

Figures

Table

Acknowledgements

This book came together as a result of ongoing research conducted by the Connected Learning Research Network, led by Mimi Ito. As the research in that network progressed, the three authors of this book realised that there was a significant gap in the research between claims made of the benefits and opportunities provided in out-of-school creative learning spaces and study of pathways young people who attended those spaces could then follow into employment. This was the genesis of our project. We want to thank the other members of the network (Richard Arum, Dalton Conley, Kris Gutiérrez, Sonia Livingstone, Vera Michalchik, Bill Penuel, Kylie Peppler, Nichole Pinkard, Jean Rhodes, Juliet Schor and Amanda Wortman), for their contributions to the discussion during various meetings over the last five years to this volume.

Julian Sefton-Green would like to thank all the individuals who contributed their time and enthusiasm in talking with him, as well as Celia Greenwood and Camille Curtis y van Dyke at WAC Arts. He would also like to thank Callum Lee and Paul Owens from BOP Consulting who helped broker the study at the British Film Institute summer programme (Chapter 5) and Pete Fraser and Jenny Grahame who helped find contacts for that work, as did Alicia Blum-Ross. Special thanks to Sonia Livingstone and Paige Mustain from the London School of Economics & Political Science who supported early work on this project.

S. Craig Watkins would also like to thank the team of researchers, designers, and media makers who supported his fieldwork, which is highlighted in some of the chapters in the book, including Andres Lombana-Bermudez, Alexander Cho, Krishnan Vasudevan, Robyn Keith, Robin McDowell, and Monique Walton.

Ben Kirshner would like to thank the youth organisations that participated in the Connected Learning Youth Researcher project, specifically the talented staff and youth researchers who explored topics related to connected learning, creative industries, and youth program quality. Ben Kirshner would also like to thank CLRN collaborators at CU Boulder, including Adam York, Josephina Chang-Order, Michael Harris, Katie

Van Horne, Erica Van Steenis, Daniela DiGiacomo, Carrie Allen, Kris Gutiérrez, and Bill Penuel.

Many thanks to the editorial team at Routledge for their patience and support during the writing of this book. Thank also to Helen Nixon for her help in the preparation of the manuscript.

This book is based on a research project supported by the John D. & Catherine T. MacArthur Foundation under Prime Award no. 10–97572–000-USP and the Regents of the University of California. Any opinions, findings, and conclusions or recommendations expressed in this publication are those of the authors and do not necessarily reflect the views of the John D. & Catherine T. MacArthur Foundation or the Regents of the University of California.

A Note on Authorship

This book came together as a result of our joint participation in the 'Connected Learning Research Network.' We devised the key research questions, as outlined in Chapter 1 and developed our individual research programmes very much in collaboration with each other as a joint effort. We shared theory and developed our separate research programmes and analysis of findings together. With the exception of Chapter 6, which we commissioned deliberately to include an account of a higher education initiative; we thus consider the volume to have been put together as a jointly authored project. Nevertheless, we want to acknowledge, in several instances, that some of us needed support in carrying out and writing up the individual case studies, which is why some of the chapters have additional co-author attributions as well as noting the lead author for each chapter.

Contributors

Josephina Chang-Order is a doctoral candidate at the University of Colorado Boulder, USA.

Phil Graham is a professor and head of School, Creative Industries at the University of the Sunshine Coast in Queensland, Australia.

Michael Harris is a PhD candidate at the University of Colorado Boulder School of Education and is currently serving as an assistant principal at an Oklahoma high school.

Ben Kirshner is Professor of Education at the University of Colorado Boulder and Faculty Director of CU Engage: Center for Community-Based Learning and Research, USA.

Andres Lombana-Bermudez is an assistant professor of communication at the Universidad Javeriana, Colombia.

Julian Sefton-Green is Professor of New Media Education at Deakin University, Australia.

Katie Van Horne is a learning scientist and an independent research and strategy consultant.

S. Craig Watkins is Founding Director of the Institute for Media Innovation and the incoming Ernest S. Sharpe Centennial Professor in the Moody College of Communication at the University of Texas at Austin, USA.

Adam York is a research associate with the National Education Policy Center, University of Colorado Boulder, USA.

1 Young People's Journeys Into Creative Work

Challenges and Transitions Into the Workforce

Julian Sefton-Green, S. Craig Watkins, and Ben Kirshner

Introduction

Over the last few years, we talked with an extraordinary range of young people with creative interests in film, art, games, hip-hop, and music who were trying to make their way in the cities of Austin, Denver, Brisbane, and London. At the same time, a persistent national and international debate about the composition of the creative labour force was taking place, backstage, as it were. Public debate about who makes up the creative labour force has been intense. Throughout 2016, outrage at the lack of representation by black actors and filmmakers led to #oscarssowhite. In the UK, the news drew attention to ways that nepotism and unfair internships have created a 'pandemic lack of inclusion'[1] in terms of people from working-class backgrounds or those discriminated against by gender or race. Academic research from 2015[2] to 2018 kept in the public eye questions about the lack of diversity both onstage and offstage, on-screen and offscreen.[3] The Hollywood film director, Paul Greengrass, proclaimed 'young people starting out in film or TV are being screwed to the ground.'[4] Since 2014, the tech industry has come under increasing scrutiny for its lack of racial, ethnic, and gender diversity (Miller, 2014). As tech, big data, and artificial intelligence become the dominant features of modern society, the lack of diversity in the design of the smart future is deeply problematic. In Australia, research highlighted gender inequality: 'women aren't the problem in the film industry, men are.'[5] Although the #metoo movement is by no means confined to media, cinema, or other creative occupations, some of its most public success has been in drawing attention to structural inequality and oppression, particularly through Time's Up.[6] Creative work, of course, extends far beyond the legacy media of film and television, and now includes digital media, design, and even the civic sphere (Watkins, 2019).

In some ways, discussion about who gets to make the media that millions of people consume has always been a fraught political question given that there is a deep common sense yoking together the idea that the way media represent diverse social groupings must in some ways be understood in terms of who makes the products in the first place (Oakley & O'Brien, 2016; Saha, 2017). Getting into the film, television, design, or tech industries is thus part of a wider social struggle for representation which in turn affects recognition of inequality and social injustice.

Of course, describing these wider debates of national cultural importance as backstage or offscreen to the discussions we were having with the young people trying to get their first exhibition or hustling to secure a DJ gig in a club in downtown Austin, Texas, might seem the wrong way around. This book focuses on the experiences of young people as they maneuvered to enter varied and changing forms of employment across the creative industries—we offer cases in film, hip-hop, game design, music, and visual arts—and our attention is on the struggle and hustle of youth as they tried to set up companies, snaffle gigs, make pitches, earn a living, or just earn respect. On the one hand, their stories are a key part of these wider debates about representation and recognition. Indeed, our young people are often precisely the segment of the workforce that appears to be more often denied equal advancement than their more privileged peers. On the other hand, whilst our criticism of the wider context certainly animated our research, the wider political canvas was not our starting point.

The book brings together a rather under-researched intersection of several fields relating to youth, employment in the creative industries, and transitions into work given that there has been a structural realignment of pathways into employment more generally (Furlong & Cartmel, 2006). While previous eras were characterised by relatively straightforward transitions from education into employment, today's youth face an extraordinary set of social challenges in terms of accessing secure employment, housing, and other opportunities to enable them to enter adult life. Indeed, assumptions about vocational pathways and full employment have been thrown into disarray as the new precarity facing the current generations has given rise to new forms of existential angst manifest in changing subjectivity, especially in relation to the extended nature of learning to work.

There are curious gaps in the research about the transitions for young people into work. This is partly a question of disciplinary provenance. Studies of education and training pay attention to credentials, outcomes, stratification, and equity. Studies of the workplace are interested in career progression, changing occupations, structures of the firm and workplace, and the impact of changing technologies. Sociological studies of youth pay attention to changing trends in employment, family, housing, and financial independence. However, given a context where all of these transitions are themselves changing in deep and essential ways, there is surprisingly little research about how young people navigate entry to employment where the concept of work might be best thought of as a *process* which might well take place over an extended period of time and across multiple pathways (Tomlinson, 2013). Given the structural decline of the long-term career, the work required to enter *work* calls for its own scholarly attention, including new understandings of work-based identity, opportunity, experience, accreditation, and both formal and informal markets.

In this book, we consider how young people enter into and navigate these new activities and its implications for the changing world of work, opportunity, and mobility. Nowhere is this more apparent than in the creative and cultural sector where traditionally high-status and difficult to enter occupations have been fundamentally restructured due to the disruptive effects of digital technologies. Far from lessening the attractions of working in these industries with their high degree of staff turnover, capricious audiences and high-risk rewards, opportunities for creative work have multiplied in recent years. Digital technologies make possible new markets and new opportunities for entrepreneurs and innovation. In the case of game development, for example, new advances in software make it possible to produce high-quality, playable games with very little money. In these and other instances, technology lowers the barrier to entry, opening up spaces for creators to make and distribute their creative work. How young people leverage emerging technologies into career and creative opportunities is one of the aims of this book.

The young people who are able to take advantage of these changes and opportunities customarily have high levels of formal education and are from affluent middle-class households with particular kinds of social and cultural capital. This raises questions about social justice and the wider social impact of control of media industries by these elites. The case studies in this book take these challenges and this inequality as their starting point and explore both how young people make and take opportunities for themselves in these precarious times of shifting structural patterns of company and employment, and, at the same time, how education and training systems, and informal innovation ecosystems, attempt to intervene in these new labour markets through forms of support, incubation, and training.

The three lead authors of this book came together as part of the Connected Learning Research Network, an interdisciplinary research group examining interest-driven learning communities, with a particular interest in how digital tools create possibilities for transforming educational opportunity for young people from socially marginalised backgrounds (Ito et al., 2013). We come from different academic disciplines, including sociology, media and communication studies, youth development, and education and cultural studies, and so arrived at our interest in the experience of transitioning into work in the creative industries from different perspectives, research traditions, and even purposes.

Defining the Field: Contexts, Approaches, and Traditions

We are united by a common political interest in using academic research to support changes in both policy and practice to improve opportunities for those young people who typically do not benefit from the current education system. Where our work is rooted in the tradition of social critique, we hope that bringing young people's accounts to the forefront will influence public debate and social expectations in relation to recruitment, sponsorship, and the provision of opportunity. Our work is also rooted in traditions of social intervention; we hope this work will contribute to changes in how higher education and non-profit organisations design outreach programmes and interventions to support young people's pathways into creative work.

We do not necessarily share a common intellectual frame defining a single problem because of the ways that the phenomenon of transitioning into work are viewed analytically by our varied disciplinary outlooks. The phenomenon represents, for example, a way of talking about managing economic precarity as much as it does forms of apprenticeship learning. These two perfectly valid insights into our young people's journeys are captured in the accounts we give but with distinct conceptual frames and disciplinary purposes. This section thus attempts to presents an overview of the range of disciplinary perspectives employed in our accounts and attempts to explore the theoretical connections (and disjuncture) as we have tried to capture a very broad process of both provision and change at work across three continents.

Creative Labour in Precarious Times

For young people today in general, transitioning into the labour market is a protracted, fraught, competitive, and precarious process. Whilst the idea of a smoothly regulated passage from training to employment carefully and fairly regulated by the acquisition of credentials may be more of a nostalgic ideal than an accurate representation of how life was lived, it is generally accepted that current times pose very different challenges for young people from all social classes (Brown, Lauder, & Ashton, 2011). Global competition, automation, AI (artificial intelligence), de-industrialisation, and regional economic inequalities have to some degree broken the compact between education and employment with a whole range of associated social consequences (Baldwin, 2016; Rifkin, 2001; Saxenian, 2006; Srnicek & Williams, 2016). Within this broader context of the changing relationship between education and work, and indeed the meaning of work itself in terms of career progression (Tomlinson, 2013), creative labour (and we shall come to challenges in this definition next) is of interest to sociologists of work very much in terms of acting ahead of its time: in Sandra Haukka's words, 'Pathways into the creative industries are not institutionally or occupationally determined compared to pathways into other industries' (Haukka, 2011, p. 6)

First of all, creative labour captures both subjective and objective dimensions to changes in the nature of work itself. There are a number of strands here. Critiques of the post-war Fordist labour markets (even when they were working successfully within their own terms in the countries of the global North) have pointed to the contradictory aesthetic and affective dimensions to the meaning of work that have been contained and incorporated as workplaces themselves, and how attitudes towards work have changed since the 1960s (Boltanski & Chiapello, 2007). Further exploration, especially associated with the work of Richard Sennett (Sennett, 2007; Sennett & Cobb, 1973), has moved our understanding of work away from a simple version of the exchange of labour to embrace subjective understandings of class consciousness and individual respect. Subsequent research into what motivates artists and other forms of creative workers has built on this tradition, showing that people who work creatively (often very broadly defined) are as much motivated by existential questions of what gives meaning to their lives in contradistinction to a narrow view of work which is solely and exclusively concerned with economic return. The work of Angela McRobbie, for example, has consistently explored the interplay of gender, class, and other meaning-making processes that can explain some of the contradictions inherent in creative labour (McRobbie, 2015).

One of the key contradictions is the classic tension between working for art or money (Taylor & Littleton, 2008a), and this theme has been stimulated by changes in the labour market more generally, summed up in the term, *precarity*. Whilst in some ways, as earlier scholars have argued, there has always been inbuilt insecurity implicit in the concept of creative work, changes in employment more generally have made creative work emblematic of broader shifts in labour practices (Standing, 2016). Precarity describes a complex process of labour market instability, undermining job security, and employment practices. However, as a number of scholars have noted, in some ways, these broader conditions have always been in force in the creative and arts sectors (Neff, Wissinger, & Zukin, 2005; Christopherson, 2006).

As we will discuss next, the emergence of precariousness as a more normal state of being clearly has significant consequences for young people as they enter into work in every field. Here, we were interested in the ways that trying to become a filmmaker, hip-hop artist, game developer, or musician might be understood in terms of choices between equally insecure options as opposed to the paradigm of art versus money, which wrongly implies that there are more sensible and safe alternatives to pursuing an artistic life. At the same time as intra-institutional studies might be able to delineate different kinds of career building (Ashton, 2015a; Felstead et al., 2007), thus shedding light on varied ways that workers are developing routes through precarity, so we wanted to explore how, faced with this norm, young people build strategies and practices to ease and safeguard their progress, such as Nelligan's study of networking in Australia opened up (Nelligan, 2015).

Studies in the US context have also examined how young people navigate these conditions of economic uncertainty through aspirational labour (Neff, 2012; Duffy, 2017), networking (Currid, 2008), and side hustling (Ravenelle, 2019; Watkins, 2019). Indeed, the latter, side hustling, has become a common feature among young people as they seek to balance the realities of having to maintain some form of employment—a day gig—while pursuing more desirable forms of employment—a side gig (Watkins, 2019).

Indeed, precarity itself is a state of economic and social relationships that are highly influenced by contingent local circumstances and subject to broader shifts. Central here is the unequal impact of digital technologies which have both transformed working practices within the specific sub-sectors of the cultural industries (Huws, 2007)—changing what it means to become an editor and so forth—and led to a democratisation of production opportunities and the growth of informal media economies (Lobato, Thomas, & Hunter, 2011). Sperlich's study of several media industries in Austria, for example, has shown how changes in technology may have driven down costs and thus had an impact on the structure of firms and media industries, but the increased costs on workers in terms of changing specialised labour skills and the contraction of protected 'work time' have all had extremely mixed effects (Sperlich, 2011).

The context for our small-scale investigations is thus quite large. We relate more general shifts in what is at stake in becoming a creative worker to the fraught nature of creative work itself with its roots in forms of unpaid and immaterial labour (as explored quite extensively in the literature around creative work, Gill & Pratt, 2008)—where benefits to the individual may only serve the larger interests of capital in whose interests precarity operates (Kennedy, 2011; Ashton, 2015b).

Becoming a Creative Worker: Identities and the Role of Formal Education

The term creative labour or creative work is deliberately ambiguous, relating to both work in formally defined creative fields (mainly the arts) and/or work which in and of itself could be intrinsically considered creative (Oakley, 2009). This double focus has had a significant impact on research into creative and cultural work, examining both the ways that training in higher education institutions geared towards specific industry-employment outcomes do and do not connect with the training and education of people who might work creatively in fields that are not defined as such (Ashton, 2015a). Policy interventions in the UK geared towards optimising the relationship between education, training, and economic productivity—especially in the earlier years of this century where the creative and cultural industries were seen as particular and privileged spaces for growth—have been vexed by this challenge[7] (see also the studies collected in Ashton & Noonan, 2013). In the US context, higher education training for industries such as film, television, music, and games has been uneven and in some cases only recently available.

Research around conservatories and higher education institutions actually responsible for the production of workers in the creative industries has, by contrast, been interested in questions concerning the promulgation of cultural norms, the capacity to build resilient portfolio careers, and, indeed, the role of social capital as ways to facilitate career progression. Kate Oakley's study of art schools and their role in producing certain kinds of sensibilities, especially in relationship to social mobility for people from working-class backgrounds (Banks & Oakley, 2015; Oakley, 2009), concluded that art schools' contemporary market orientation has influenced the range of add-on and follow-up practices they now offer. Ashton's (2013) study of nascent creatives in higher education examines how curriculum attempts to replicate 'authentic' work and Petrie's history of production training in film education as it became institutionalised under a national push to exploit creative industries over the last 20 years (Petrie, 2012) all explore the intricate ways that educational institutions work to offer graduates modes of identity and behaviour deemed acceptable by current industry practices (see also Mayer, Banks, & Caldwell, 2009; Mayer, 2011). Whereas, for example, some of the work of Angela McRobbie discussed earlier looked at questions of identity as produced through work itself, these scholars have explored the ways that institutions have tried to 'reverse engineer' the findings of such cultural theory and thus seek to 'produce' students with certain kinds of identities.

More intensive research into the ways that identities themselves are formed beyond the desirable dispositions advocated by training institutions can be found in the extensive analysis of workers by Taylor and Littleton (Taylor & Littleton, 2008b, 2016). Some of our studies in this book have been inspired by this approach, which has examined the discourses around artistic identity and the ways that these are mobilised in terms of narratives of the self and in context with specific projects, creative output, and, indeed, creative biography accounts. Again, picking up from theoretical interest in dispositions—part of McRobbie's theoretical repertoire to explain the intersection between market opportunity, individual life choice, and creative work—Taylor and Littleton show how creative work is valued by artists/practitioners as much for its non-instrumental value as its earnings-related possibilities. This kind of approach also helps us understand how individuals navigate difficult and changing circumstances, creating a stable identity across fluid and challenging life circumstances. Such an approach has been helpful as we have looked to see how young people create these identities for themselves, let alone begin to sustain them across the life course.

As a result of our work with the Connected Learning Research Network, we are also sensitive to the notion that informal learning practices and ecosystems are crucial to understanding both how and where young people learn (Ito et al., 2013). In short, learning how to do creative labour has a long history outside of formal schooling institutions. Young people have been especially creative in designing their own places to learn the skills that are key to pursuing creative work. Thus, some of the chapters discussed next, such as the exploration of independent game developers and aspiring hip-hop artists, focus on informal innovation ecosystems and the informal modes of learning that have only become more crucial in the context of escalating college costs and historic debts (Selingo, 2013; Taylor, Fry, & Oates, 2014).

Creative and Cultural Industries: Sectors and Fields

Although the term creative labour can be used to describe work taking place outside of any economic sectors that are described as creative, for the purposes of the studies in this book, we are interested in employment in what has been called both the creative and cultural industries. At the outset, it is worth noting that we are not interested in the routes taken by young people getting jobs in non-creative occupations in those industries (this definitional problem has been important in much of the creative economy literature [Bilton, 2006]). The distinction between the language of creative and cultural industries and the arts is a testimony to an important debate about cultural value where being involved in the arts spoke to a pre-industrialised model of creative production that aspired to evade any notion of economic utility (Belfiore & Bennett, 2007; Carey, 2006). Again, that argument is not one we pursue in this book, even if it informs discourses around creative identities as described earlier.

Sociological studies of creative production, especially those examining the production, circulation, and reception of products as part of any economy, have been indebted to the work of Howard Becker and his characterisation of art worlds (Becker, 1984). His approach to creative production as a many-levelled, collaborative economic enterprise existing within specific markets, and concerned with the maintenance and regulation of economic as well as aesthetic value has had an enormous impact on studies of creative production. Studies of the film sector (for example, Caves, 2000; Caldwell, 2008), visual arts (Thornton, 2009), and so forth all draw on ideas of creative labour as specific kinds of employment relationships. Broad understandings of cultural industries from a critical perspective (Adorno, 1991) have fused with growing awareness of the economic potential of the cultural industries during the 1990s (Hartley, 2004), leading to a firm rejection of the arts paradigms in favour of an understanding of the creative industries and their part in the burgeoning knowledge economy of the information society (Huws, 2007). The work of Richard Florida has had significant traction at the policy-making level (Florida, 2002). Florida's work has been taken up by cities using creative industries as a lever for urban regeneration. From our point of view, this aspect to the confluence of scholarly fields has two main interests. First of all, following the work of Florida, and indeed understanding the creative industries as an economic driver for growth, we can see that many of the young people we studied in our cities were seizing opportunities and participating in emerging markets as part of city-led modes of growth and transformation. At a social level, this has significant consequences for young people from marginalised communities within struggles related to gentrification in the city (Krytyka Polityczna & European Cultural Foundation, 2015). The chapters in this volume looking at independent game developers and hip-hop artists explore how urban transformation and gentrification have forced young people to be more inventive, not only in terms of how they pursue creative work but also where they pursue creative work. In his analysis of what he calls young creatives, Watkins (2019) analyses how they fashion their own innovation economy in part by adopting non-conventional spaces, such as coworking spaces, coffee shops, old buildings, an apartment, and event spaces to expand the geography of innovation. Secondly, interest in the preparation of young people for participation in these burgeoning and changing markets can be found in many initiatives and educational interventions that are supported by public and philanthropic funding to bring about social change. A third, and more distant interest for this volume is the literature analysing differential opportunities in the different subsectors that comprise the creative economy (Higgs & Cunningham, 2007). Although not of direct concern to us, it's fair to say that much of the literature around specific labour markets is derived from an interest in analysing supply and demand at a local sub-sectorial level, and this does have some influence on the kinds of opportunities that are available in any one particular location.

In the UK, for example, there has been particular specific interest in developing talent and opportunity in digital industries[8] and studies of creative labour are often analysed within the context of sub-sectorial constraints. Livermore's Canada-based thesis looking at opportunities and use of creative labour in the game industry (Livermore, 2013; see also Sefton-Green & Brown, 2014) are examples of the ways that study of young people's transitions into employment is very much framed by the particular logic and constraints of the ways that specific industries operate in particular locations. In the US, debates about the lack of workforce diversity in science, technology, engineering, and mathematics (STEM) occupations related to creative work—game development, digital media, and AI—have sparked a number of efforts among non-profit organisations to expose diverse youth to skills, such as coding, design, and entrepreneurship (Ito et al., 2013). In addition, many young people have responded to the lack of a diverse workforce in the STEM economy by doing what schools have been unable to do: develop initiatives and opportunities that cultivate a more diverse pipeline of tech talent (Watkins, 2019).

Youth Cultures and Youth Transitions

The scholarship around creative labour and the creative workforce has stemmed from a disciplinary interest in the sociology of work. But given Steven Threadgold's observation that there are 'two camps in the sociological study of youth: youth cultures and youth transitions' (Threadgold, 2017, p. 11), it has to some extent been the youth culture's tradition that has also underpinned investigations in creative labour, as exemplified in the scholarship of Angela Robbie. The youth culture's tradition has explored the organisation, performance, and, especially, the visual (spectacular) identities of young people and highly visible subcultural expressions. Thus, now classic studies of, for example, punk (Hebdige, 1979), did not only focus on behaviour, music, or public visibility but also drew attention to both the cultures of learning and, indeed, the commodification of punk culture as part of the investigation of subculture itself. Analysis of style is inevitably implicated in a study of the marketplace and so, as with other genres or subcultures such as hip-hop or club culture (Thornton, 1995), scholarship has examined the ways in which the practices of culture equally exemplify the development of enterprise, hustle, and marketisation. In turn, investigations of the practices of youth subcultures have become abstracted to focus on more general aspects of what might be at stake in becoming a creative worker and especially where entrepreneurial drive has given birth to forms of DIY culture (Threadgold, 2017; Bennett, 2017).

Although many cultural and subcultural activities take place in informal economies and often comprise a hinterland to mainstream economic activity, this strand in youth cultures' research has paid attention to the nature of work—for example, in studies of aspirant musicians and gigging in local economies (Finnegan, 2007; Bartleet, Bennett, & Bridgstock, 2012). Scholarship here had already begun to investigate the meaning of 'immaterial labour' (Terranova, 2004) in predigital contexts. Indeed, some of the art versus money kind of dilemmas discussed in the literature earlier, and additionally the focus on existential satisfaction, have derived from this tradition. Thus, for example, studies of advertising (Nixon, 2003), film and television (Hesmondhalgh & Baker, 2011), or the arts (Currid, 2008), which situate themselves significantly in the field of the sociology of work, draw on models of apprenticeship, informal economy, and entrepreneurial hustle or DIY as ways to explain what motivates individuals and how they piece together trajectories into work that derives from academic scholarship in the youth cultures tradition. The study of youth cultures is, of course, inseparable from broader study around the changing nature of youth transitions and indeed originated in analysis of the production of post-war youth culture as a specific life stage (Griffin, 1993). The focus on youth transitions is, of course, a move from dependency on the family to adulthood and has especially paid attention to what is at stake in achieving economic independence. In the US, scholars have focused on how shifting social, economic, educational, and policy currents have reshaped young people's transition to adulthood while also highlighting the unique challenges faced by youth from under-resourced schools, households, and communities. This body of research poses a question that is central to our work as well: are some young people at greater risk of failure in the transition from student to independent worker and young adulthood (Donahoe & Tienda, 2000)? Some of the chapters in this volume suggest that while young people in general face economic precarity, some young people are especially vulnerable in light of the resource disparities in social, economic, and human capital. In the US, for example, researchers have focused on the challenges that young African Americans and Latinos face in terms of educational attainment and occupational employment (Jones & Schmitt, 2014).

Recent scholarship on youth transitions has been vexed by the breakdown in clear life-stage demarcated institutional frames—family, work, and so forth. Indeed, as a wide range of studies have shown, the lack of secure stable employment and the inability of societies in the global North to plan and control demand in the labour market (Brown et al., 2011) in ways that seemed to operate for previous generations has led to a series of crises for contemporary youth (Howker & Malik, 2013). These revolve around changes in the value of accreditation for entry into the labour market, the breakdown of employment-for-life single employer models, and access to housing. Yet again, we have to consider how this broader context affects our more specific focus. For example, Lalley and Doyle draw a range of international comparative examples to show how the idea of preparatory training for employment (as offered through accredited courses in conventional colleges and academic institutions) has now broadened to include forms of contextually specific and informal educational opportunities, as well as a raft of blended kinds of learning so that the idea of a transition from an educational institution into a place of work can now be theorised and understood as taking place over a longer period of time and in a far less stepped pre- and post-statutory education model (Lally & Doyle, 2012).

In applying these more general perspectives to make sense of entry into the creative industries, Haukka argues that, first of all, we are faced with a methodological problem of the fact that the creative sector (when considered a discrete or distinctive future of the economy) is extremely difficult to measure, as noted in comments earlier about whether creative work refers to employment in the arts or all work that is in itself creative. A consequence here is that research in this area is often extremely difficult to carry out because of the challenge in defining economic sub-sectors. Secondly, Haukka suggests that the creative industries are less driven by credentials than other employment sectors. Thirdly, the fluidity of transitions and non-linear career pathways means that the return on investment and utility of higher education qualifications is not simple to calculate, prepare for, or, indeed, organise. And fourth, work in the creative sector is often flexible, mobile, and collaborative, thus exacerbating difficulties in definition, planning, and supplying labour (Haukka, 2011). In general, then, close examination of transition into work in the creative sector both advances and reforms our understanding of what transitions could mean in principle. The transitions literature which explores the structural social conditions changing opportunities for young people in general is helpful for understanding the kinds of options youth might be experiencing at the same time as its application to exploring transition into employment in a specific field—here defined quite broadly in terms of creative work—requires reflexive interpretation as the process of transition itself both exacerbates and/or is transformed by these larger structural conditions.

Education, Training, and Interventions

The final key theme in our matrix of influences derives from the field of education. As we have already observed in discussions about the development of creative identities, the discourse of being a creative worker and how that is taught and sponsored, especially by conservatories and higher education (HE) institutions, is an important constituent element in the make-up of creative labour. Education in creative fields is clearly more than simply the acquisition of discrete production skills and, as the contributors to a 2013 volume (Ashton & Noonan, 2013) attest, includes examination of the interface between training and internships/work placements, management of portfolio careers (especially with an attention to the management of professional behaviours), questions about gender, race, and, indeed, the inculcation of practice from industry experience. Examining the ways that institutional validation both includes and excludes individuals, as well as reflecting on the kinds of knowledge that need to form part of the education for a creative worker, inform several contributions to this volume as well. In particular, we pick up Angela Robbie's interest in dispositions (McRobbie, 2015) and Taylor and Littleton's characterisation of identity (Taylor & Littleton, 2016) as openings to explore the weave of aesthetic values, existential reflexivity, and exploitation of context-specific opportunity, all of which are frames very much derived from their incorporation as legitimate ways of being through forms of graduation and accreditation.

The interface between HE and industry/employment is, however, only one part of the picture and has, as already suggested, comprised the material for a distinctive research field. The relationship between school-level education and transitioning into the workplace in this specific sector, and indeed the role of out-of-school initiatives and their interrelationships with employment, has not received the same amount of scholarly attention, and this volume aims to remediate that absence.

There are several obvious reasons why pre-HE/training is not usually taken into consideration when exploring transitions into creative work. First of all is the fact that despite observations like Haukka's noted earlier about a lack of reliance on qualifications in the creative industries, this does not mean that most creative workers are not graduates: indeed, in the context of the oversupply of qualified labour[9]—a problem that is even more acute in the creative sector—it is not usual for young people to transition directly from school into these workplaces. Secondly, the fields of creative production do not normally have correspondence with the standard academic curriculum, and, again, further specialised training is the norm. However, whereas the transitions literature tends to focus on the extension of the transition throughout the young person's 20s and perhaps even into their 30s, one logic of the conceptual movement in such literature is also to direct attention to the transition as taking place at a younger age, as it were. In other words, young people need to be at a certain kind of stage before they even get to HE and, indeed, reconceptualising transition as an ongoing process rather than a simple movement between fixed positions also means that we need to think about the ways that young people learn to become creative workers throughout their educational formation.

Take, for example, the ethnographic work of Watkins et al. (2018) on the challenges schools face in trying to prepare a more diverse population of youth for work in the creative tech sector. Similar to other accounts, they found that even as more technology, such as computers, tablets, software, and the Internet, is pouring into schools populated by youth from lower-income households, the opportunity for these students to learn valuable skills remains limited. Schools, they argue, are technology rich but curriculum poor—a condition found by Margolis (2008) and her colleagues in a study of high school computer science courses. In other words, even as schools recognise the need to invest more of their resources into STEM literacy, the approach taken with black and Latino students tends to emphasise rudimentary technical skills (i.e. search, PowerPoint, graphics) rather than more nuanced academic and design skills (i.e. coding, inquiry, prototyping). The latter skills correlate more positively with the evolving demands of an economy driven by computerisation and automation (Levy & Murnane, 2004).

There are very few accounts taking such a perspective. One exception comes from interest in 'technobiographies' among learning scientists (Miller, Henwood, & Kennedy, 2001; Barron, Gomez, Pinkard, &

Martin, 2014), which has been developed into a biographical account of the growth of digital creatives (Sefton-Green & Brown, 2014). Whilst narrative biographies of established artists will recount stories of the early formation through schooling, it has mainly been in the science and technology (STEM) field that research has been conducted on how schooling in academic subjects might orientate individuals towards dispositions and life-course decisions and trajectories (Bell, Leah, Reeve, & Tzou, 2012; Stevens, O'Connor, Garrison, Jocuns, & Amos, 2008). It is, of course, concern with the underrepresentation of both women and ethnic minorities (just like the creative sector) and a wider concern with STEM pathways that frames such research but, nevertheless, there are principles about the ways that individual youth interest is captured, mediated, mentored, and progressed that can be extrapolated for creative labour. A point of difference between STEM and creative fields is, of course, the seemingly specialised progression routes required in STEM. Yet some of the studies collected here, and indeed the accounts from HE already discussed, show that such forms of identity specialisation occur, whatever the trajectory.

A significant area of interest in the ways that out-of-school interest can be leveraged to further longer-term career trajectories has also focused on the provision and value of organised out-of-school, non-formal learning (Sefton-Green, 2013). Interest in out-of-school, informal, or non-formal provision intersects with this research in a number of ways. First of all is the focus on supporting interest-driven learning, especially where it has a route in the young person's frequently marginalised culture (Barron et al., 2014). Secondly, out-of-school learning has often been proposed as an intervention in areas of high economic disadvantage and attention to culturally driven activities that are often proposed as ways of recruiting young people back into education in general. They also exhibit forms of pedagogy and student engagement frequently absent from mainstream education (Watkins et al., 2018; Kirshner, 2015; Soep & Chavez, 2010). Thirdly, the role of new and emerging forms of culture from the street is often managed as a way of revitalising forms of culture more generally. Fourth, out-of-school learning is often proposed as a way of resolving a number of social problems with youth (Poyntz et al., 2019). And, finally, it should be noted that informal learning opportunities are often sites for the development of new and changing cultural practices before they become incorporated in the regular academic curriculum (Dewdney & Lister, 1988).

Many of these interests in the out-of-school learning space do, of course, have intense points of connection with the youth cultures and youth subculture literature and thus feed into a concern with developing young people's participation in expressive cultures, even if the focus from this perspective is not necessarily how to turn such participation into forms of work. The practices of out-of-school learning also offer complementary strategies to both make sense of and support young people's journeys into creative work.

Our Research Questions

The Connected Learning Research Network, which sponsored our work, became interested in the journey from education into work and, more precisely, opportunity. Our concern with interest-driven learning and the role of both digital technologies and out-of-school informal learning environments focused on the ways that the provision of such forms of education might support different kinds of economic opportunity for socially and politically marginalised young people. As we began to look at young people transitioning into work in the creative sectors, as they aspired to and learnt to become part of the creative workforce, we realised that even though we were looking at very different cases in various cities around the world, we were asking a core set of questions deriving from the academic landscape we have just described.

First of all, we wanted to characterise the agency of young people themselves. Discussions about creative labour and transitions to employment tend to underplay individual and collective enterprise, entrepreneurialism, and the capacity of 'hustle' to renegotiate dominant social structures and systems. Secondly, we recognised that insights into social injustice coming out of a critique of current education systems and the creative and cultural industries did not accommodate the raft of initiatives, interventions, and projects that have been set up and are supported around the world to offer young people—frequently from socially marginalised backgrounds—the kinds of opportunities, networks, and relationships that are usually taken for granted by their more privileged peers. These two perspectives, young people's agency and the varied potential of organised 'interventions,' order the arrangement of the chapters in this volume.

The main discussion in this chapter has been to show the relationships between the key academic traditions that we attempt to bring together in our case studies. In summary, our case studies took up these challenges.

- In respect of general arguments around precarity: how does entry into informal media economies in local markets advance our understanding of how young people are navigating precarity? In what ways do more general states of precariousness in terms of understanding possible futures and the labour market influence senses of possibility and opportunity in new kinds of creative media making?
- In respect of questions about how people 'become' creative workers: what ways are notions of identity, taste, and social class important to how young people 'become' creative workers? What are the relationships between formal education, cultural capital, and psychosocial processes at work as people learn to become 'creatives'?

- In relationship to questions about what comprises the field of creative work we ask, are there differences between becoming a creative worker in one field (or economic sub-sector) or another? In what ways have changes in production technology, especially digital technologies, affected field-specific understandings of and entry into, creative work? What is the relationship between creative economy, urban regeneration, and opportunities for youth? How does a rapidly evolving technology landscape both lower the barrier to entry into creative work and make 'success' more challenging at the same time?
- What is the relationship between creative economy, urban regeneration, and opportunities for youth? How is the remaking of cities opening up new spaces and opportunities, often unintentionally, that expand the geography of innovation in ways that drive young people's desire to pursue more creative forms of work?
- And in relationship to questions about youth cultures and youth transitions, we are interested in the question, how does an understanding of youth cultures help us make sense of changing labour markets and their possibilities? Is employment in the changing nature of the creative economy really supporting or hindering the experiences of transition into employment?
- Finally, in respect to education, and especially the whole field of out-of-school learning, we wanted to know, in what ways do forms of learning and mentoring (pedagogy), especially in non-formal and out-of-school projects and interventions, create the conditions to support young people, especially those from socially marginalised backgrounds, to enter into the creative workforce?

The book offers insight into how young people connect to opportunity in a society and economy defined by significant social, economic, and technological change. As the world of work becomes more precarious and unfulfilling, a growing number of young people are seeking alternative pathways to work that are rewarding, fulfilling, and entrepreneurial. In our cases, entrepreneurial practices are not necessarily about the pursuit of wealth but rather the freedom to engage in creative endeavours that are rewarding and afford more agency in defining young people's lives and their careers. Still, the journey into work that is alternative and creative is marked by many challenges, most notably limited resources.

The Organisation of This Book

Chapter 2 profiles an ecosystem that fosters the development of independent games. Relying mainly on access to relatively cheap tools, new distribution platforms, and distributed labour, this group of developers has fashioned a viable alternative economy for making games. Chapter 3 focuses on a hip-hop collective made up largely of 'aspirational labour.' This particular ecosystem consists of rappers, beat makers, producers, and artists who aspire to break into the music industry as recording artists, producers, and performers. While these two ecosystems are different in many ways, they each reflect the inventive tendencies among young people to actively design pathways to pursue their creative aspirations without any significant formal or institutional support. These enterprises are made up largely of what young people call the 'side hustle'—a reference to the inventive ways young people pull together the resources they need to pursue the careers they want. In these two chapters, we explore how young people labour to cultivate key forms of capital—social, technological, physical, and human—to pursue their creative aspirations.

Social capital refers to the range of social ties and networks that are central to any innovation ecosystem. Even as young people are constantly criticised for being 'tech addicted' and antisocial, these chapters suggest something notably different—young people are extraordinarily social and constantly seek out ways to connect to others and build relationships that grow their social capital and access to both material and emotional resources (Watkins, 2019). For example, the independent game developers, described in Chapter 2, use a monthly meet-up to meet other indie developers, share their games for feedback, recruit talent, and sustain an innovation ecosystem that promotes making games. The members of the hip-hop collective, described in Chapter 3, participate in a weekly open mic night that affords artists the opportunity to test new music, get audience feedback, and connect with other music makers.

Not surprisingly, *techno-capital* is a key feature in both case studies in these opening chapters. The game developers adopt a variety of affordable software applications to make high-quality 3D games. Moreover, platforms such as Unity, YouTube, and a burgeoning app economy have forged open new spaces for the creation, distribution, and consumption of indie games. Similarly, members of the hip-hop collective (in Chapter 3) have adopted technology—laptops, smartphones, social media, and digital music applications—to participate in an underground music-making economy that allows up-and-coming musicians to make music, distribute music, and build a community around their music.

Both of these ecosystems benefitted from the use of *physical capital*, that is, spaces that are free and allow young people to make real-world connections, collaborate, share their work, and build community. In the creative world of work that young people are designing, physical capital or spaces to meet, talk, and share ideas are a crucial component in their journey to creative work. Finally, like all good innovation ecosystems, these two cases also consider how young people cultivate the skills they need to pursue work that is more creative, fulfilling, and entrepreneurial. This aspect of innovation—human capital—suggests that young people are also finding alternative ways—peers, clusters of creativity, physical spaces, and the Internet—to grow their human capital and creative potential.

Chapter 4 develops this concern with forms of social capital as it draws on a series of interviews with young people mainly in their 20s and mainly from ethnic minorities, all of whom had worked, were working as, or aspired to work as filmmakers in London in 2015/2016. It argues that rather than seeing employment in this field in simply transactional terms, as the exchange of labour in a market, it makes more sense to see these creative biographies as a form of participation in filmmaking as a social field. Having a job was understood in terms of a form of social participation which in turn generated further employment. Participation was significantly a question of identity work, of operating as a character in the social field, rather than simply a question of abstractly developing expertise (with technology or aesthetics) that could be bought or sold, and this approach to skills is in contradistinction to conventional progression through formal academic credentials. The chapter is structured around participation in three kinds of 'fields of practice' in the Bourdieuian sense. The first of these can best be described as a 'scene'—a cultural grouping or activity or performance or coming together characterised by a collective sense of purpose and engagement. Secondly, it describes young people's paid work in the film industries—that is, more conventional types of employment. These narratives showed that the market for film is varied and insecure: from public relations companies that wanted 'spontaneous' footage of events for use on Facebook, to making music videos sometimes financed by drug money, to working in a junior capacity on large Hollywood or British film industry financed films. The final kind of work we observed in these young people was the effort and process that went into the activity of career building as part of their presence in the filmmaking field. The chapter shows how young people entering this field of work have learnt to think of entry into employment not in terms of simply 'getting a job' but more in terms of monetising their participation in a series of fields.

The next set of chapters in the book changes focus from looking at the ways that young people themselves are driving change and exploiting opportunity to accounts of projects, interventions, and networks that have been set up in HE and out-of-school provision to support entry into the labour market. These initiatives have been particularly motivated by the concern for remediating social injustice.

Chapter 5 is built around a set of interviews with young people who attended the early years of a course run by the British Film Institute in England, known as the Film Academy. Despite the fact that competition for jobs in the creative and cultural industries—especially in film or TV production—is intense, and despite the fact that there is a huge pool of reserve labour often 'between jobs,' there is still significant political (and in the UK at any rate, policy) interest in developing opportunities and access for young people in these employment fields. The chapter does not evaluate the success of the intervention. It focuses on the ways that young people took up and interpreted the trajectory of becoming a filmmaker—not only suggested by participating in this course but also how these sorts of opportunities intersected with other ways of imagining a creative career. It suggests that participating in this course enabled these young people to practice new modes of careership, introducing them to ways of imagining, marking, and negotiating their futures in ways that, ironically, the rationale for the course, with its focus on introducing professional filmmaking practices, was unprepared for. It explores the contradictory relationship between the school examination system that identifies individual performance and a creative filmmaking culture that emphasises collegiality and collaboration, arguing that the young people themselves focused on forms of identity validation through peer recognition and the development of cultural capital.

Chapter 6 describes a research and engagement project through which a pedagogy of experience presented itself as a fruitful way forward for teaching creative industries professionalism in HE contexts. The project, *Indie 100*, involved hundreds of local musicians in an annual attempt to create 100 new songs in 100 hours. Following an intense week of music production, the project undertook to promote and commercialise the material over the following 12 months. During the five-year period in which the project ran, its participants—including musicians, students, and industry professionals from throughout Australia and internationally, along with staff from the university that ran the project—formed into numerous and surprising project configurations, many of which resulted in ongoing success. The historical slant of the chapter situates today's young musician within a fast-emerging, post-digital 'handicraft' economy. That is, rather than being simply an industrial hand—solely a maker of musical things—today's musician will often need to compose, record, stage, produce, release, promote, and manage the copyrights they produce, at least until they can afford to 'outsource' one or more of the functions that add up to a musical living. Or, to put it more simply, today's musician must make, promote, and sell his or her music, with all the complications that involves.

The recorded music industry is especially perplexing for young artists, in large part because of its intersection with national and international intellectual property (IP) regimes, and with a long corporate influence on the ways in which the act of making a record is understood, both in law and interpersonally. The chapter details the ways in which IP and musical aspirations redound against each other to produce the complex legal relationships involved in any recording. The chapter draws on John Dewey's emphasis on locality in his analysis of experiential learning as a way of providing a basis upon which new understandings of curriculum can emerge in a globalised semiotic environment (which includes the legal, business, and aesthetic environments) dominated by the likes of Google, YouTube, Facebook, and Instagram. The experience of *Indie 100* showed those involved how quickly and strangely the informational deluge facilitated by those behemoths has come to challenge the centuries-old 'knowledge monopoly' formerly held by universities and other institutes of higher learning. Rather than continue as brokers of 'sacred' or 'secret' information, the experience of *Indie 100* indicates the future for HE, at least in creative industries, is one in which students are guided through high-value, high-stakes, high-profile projects that immerse them in professional networks, professional working circumstances, and professional levels of intensity and engagement.

The final two chapters in the book examine structures of support and guidance from out-of-school contexts. Although a central purpose of this book is to showcase the agency and ingenuity of young people as they seek and sustain work in creative industries, these journeys into creative work are not solo projects. The research described in Chapter 7 found ubiquitous examples of key others—sometimes mentors, sometimes teachers, sometimes gatekeepers—who played critical roles in coaching young artists and brokering their access to creative networks and industries. Attention to the role of key others guiding young people's artistic pathways is important because creative fields tend to be less gated by certificates and formal school credentials, and, therefore, networks and contacts take on greater importance. Also, whereas there is a large amount of literature on the role of adults as teachers in youth development programmes, and a still vaster amount of literature on how mentoring can be a vehicle for youth development and resilience, there is far less research about the kinds of mentoring, brokering, and coaching that young people recruit in their efforts to find and sustain artistic work in creative industries, particularly once they've left programmes.

Chapter 7 draws on data from arts programmes for youth and young adults in two cities, London and Denver, to generate a typology of different kinds of guidance performed by more experienced others to support access and opportunity in the last mile. The varied origins of these data allow us to combine young people's meaning-making from interviews (London) with observations of guidance in practice (Denver). We found that some guidance in creative industries grew out of relations of care, such as with parents or educators who pushed young people to pursue new opportunities and coached them in general self-advocacy strategies, even if those caring mentors did not have extensive knowledge or access to creative industries. Young artists, of course, also placed great value on industry contacts. They described guidance embedded in shorter-duration relationships that connected, introduced, or brokered access to industry professionals and paid work. Third, we observed a key role played by those insiders who could validate the talent or vision of emerging artists. This validation, most useful when coming from industry insiders, offered confirmation of young artists' identities and commitments. Fourth, in the ecosystem of socially engaged public artists in Colorado, the practice of 'making visible' the field for young aspiring artists was important; more experienced artists showed the way by modelling an identity for youth but also breaking down the various relationships and ideologies that stitch together these diffuse or hidden networks. The chapter offers a beginning typology with the intention of generating future work that examines guidance and brokering in creative industries.

Chapter 8 takes general principles about brokering and guidance in out-of-school learning as a starting point and then compares how it might work in respect to different employment fields or sectors. Current research on learning in digital media arts programmes has documented the literacies young people practice and the forms of apprenticeship learning they experience inside high-quality programmes. What has received less attention, however, is the role that programmes can play in supporting young people in securing work or opportunity beyond the programme itself. This calls for a shift in how programmes envision their relationship with youth—from a focus on their experience within the time and space of the structured programme to a more extended relationship that supports post- programme transitions. Research about how young people construct pathways is especially needed because emerging research suggests that the new media arts domain has both a high level of openness and precarity that is distinct from other occupations, particularly those that are gated by credentials or HE degrees. In this chapter, we argue for an expanded horizon that attends to the ways that programmes might support young people in building pathways from programme participation to sustainable employment. This chapter draws on data collected from a participatory research project called Pathways, carried out with youth research teams from two programmes in the Northeast US: one with a new media arts (NMA) focus, the other with a STEM focus. Youth researchers interviewed peers and programme staff about their experiences in the programme and their understanding of pathways to future work in desired fields. Although both sites showed similar evidence of programme quality, cross-case analysis showed divergence in the availability and visibility of NMA and STEM pathways to young people. This difference was not due to differences in programme quality but instead variations in the fields. Whereas young people's narratives about STEM pursuits reflected gated, brokered, and institutionally supported pathways, stories about NMA reflected greater openness and opacity. We share examples of distinct strategies developed by both programmes to support young people in their pursuit of creative futures given these features of the ecosystem. The chapter discusses implications for work that youth initiatives must do to organise for young people's learning, not only within the setting but also in their movement into sustainable livelihoods.

Notes

1. www.theguardian.com/film/2017/jun/28/researchers-find-culture-of-nepotism-in-british-film-industry
2. www.gold.ac.uk/news/the-creative-industries-and-meritocracy/
   www.theguardian.com/culture/2015/sep/21/panic-survey-diversity-uk-arts-institutions
3. www.theguardian.com/culture/2018/apr/16/arts-industry-report-asks-where-are-all-the-working-class-people
   www.createlondon.org/panic/
4. www.theguardian.com/film/2016/apr/05/paul-greengrass-young-people-breakthrough-brits-bafta
5. https://theconversation.com/women-arent-the-problem-in-the-film-industry-men-are-68740
6. www.timesupnow.com
7. www.creativeskillseurope.eu/workforce-survey/
8. https://ccskills.org.uk/downloads/CCS_BUILDINGACREATIVENATION_WEB_SINGLES.pdf
9. www.cipd.co.uk/Images/over-qualification-and-skills-mismatch-graduate-labour-market_tcm18-10231.pdf

References

Adorno, T. (1991). *The culture industry*. London, UK: Routledge.

Ashton, D. (2013). Cultural workers in-the-making. *European Journal of Cultural Studies*, 16(4), 468–488.

Ashton, D. (2015a). Making media workers: Contesting film and television industry career pathways. *Television & New Media*, 16(3), 275–294.

Ashton, D. (2015b). Creative work careers: Pathways and portfolios for the creative economy. *Journal of Education and Work*, 28(4), 388–406.

Ashton, D., & Noonan, C. (Eds.). (2013). *Cultural work and higher education* (2013 ed.). London, UK: Palgrave Macmillan.

Baldwin, R. (2016). *The great convergence: Information technology and the new globalization*. Cambridge, MA: Harvard University Press.

Banks, M., & Oakley, K. (2015). The dance goes on forever? Art schools, class and UK higher education. *International Journal of Cultural Policy*, 22(1), 1–17.

Barron, B., Gomez, K., Pinkard, N., & Martin, C. K. (2014). *The digital youth network: Cultivating new media citizenship in urban communities*. Cambridge, MA: MIT Press.

Bartleet, B. L., Bennett, D., & Bridgstock, R. (2012). Preparing for portfolio careers in Australian music: Setting a research agenda. *Australian Journal of Music Education*, 1, 32–41.

Becker, H. S. (1984). *Art worlds*. Oakland, CA: University of California Press.

Belfiore, E., & Bennett, O. (2007). Determinants of impact: Towards a better understanding of encounters with the arts. *Cultural Trends*, 16(3), 225–275.

Bell, P., Leah, B., Reeve, S., & Tzou, C. (2012). Discovering and supporting successful learning pathways of youth in and out of school: Accounting for the development of everyday expertise across settings. In B. Bevan, P. Bell, R. Stevens, & A. Razfar (Eds.), *Lost Opportunities: Learning in out of school time*. Dordrecht: Springer. https://doi.org/10.1007/978-94-007-4304-5_9

Bennett, A. (2017). Youth, music and DIY careers. *Cultural Sociology*, 12(2), 133–139.

Bilton, C. (2006). *Management and creativity: From creative industries to creative management*. Malden, MA: Wiley-Blackwell.

Boltanski, L., & Chiapello, E. (2007). *The new spirit of capitalism*. London, UK: Verso.

Brown, P., Lauder, H., & Ashton, D. (2011). *The global auction: The broken promises of education, jobs, and incomes*. New York, NY: Oxford University Press.

Caldwell, J. T. (2008). *Production culture: Industrial reflexivity and critical practice in film and television*. Durham, NC: Duke University Press Books.

Carey, J. (2006). *What good are the arts?* London, UK: Faber and Faber.

Caves, R. E. (2000). *Creative industries: Contracts between art and commerce*. Cambridge, MA: Harvard University Press.

Christopherson, S. (2006). Behind the scenes: How transnational firms are constructing a new international division of labour in media work. *Geoforum, 37*, 739–751.

Currid, E. (2008). *The Warhol economy: How fashion, art, and music drive New York City*. Princeton, NJ: Princeton University Press.

Dewdney, A., & Lister, M. (1988). *Youth, culture and photography*. Youth questions series. London, UK: Palgrave Macmillan.

Donahoe, D., & M. Tienda. (2000). The transition from school to work: Is there a crisis? What can be done? In S. Danziger & J. Waldfogel (Eds.), *Securing the future: Investing in children from birth to college*. New York, NY: Russell Sage Foundation.

Duffy, B. E. (2017). *(Not) getting paid to do what you love: Gender, social media, and aspirational work*. New Haven, CT: Yale University Press.

Felstead, A., Bishop, D., Fuller, A., Jewson, N., Unwin, L., & Kakavelakis, K. (2007). *Performing identities at work: Evidence from contrasting sectors*. Learning as Work Research Paper, 9. Cardiff, UK: Cardiff School of Social Sciences.

Finnegan, R. (2007). *The hidden musicians: Music-making in an English town*. Music culture series. London, UK: Wesleyan University Press.

Florida, R. (2002). *The rise of the creative class: And how it's transforming work, leisure, community and everyday life*. New York, NY: Basic Books Inc.

Furlong, A., & Cartmel, F. (2006). *Young people and social change: New perspectives* (2nd ed.). Milton Keynes, UK: Open University Press.

Gill, R., & Pratt, A. (2008). In the social factory?: Immaterial labour, precariousness and cultural work. *Theory, Culture & Society, 25*(7–8), 1–30.

Griffin, C. (1993). *Representations of youth: The study of youth and adolescence in Britain and America*. Feminist perspectives series. Cambridge, UK: Polity.

Hartley, J. (2004). *Creative industries* (1st ed., Later Impression ed.). Malden, MA: Wiley-Blackwell.

Haukka, S. (2011). Education-to-work transitions of aspiring creatives. *Cultural Trends, 20*(1), 41–64.

Hebdige, D. (1979). *Subculture: The meaning of style*. New accents series. London, UK: Routledge.

Hesmondhalgh, D., & Baker, S. (2011). *Creative labour: Media work in three cultural industries*. Culture, economy and the social series. London, UK: Routledge.

Higgs, P. L., Cunningham, S., & Pagan, J. D. (2007). Australia's creative economy: Basic evidence on size, growth, income and employment. Technical Report, Faculty Research Office, CCI. http://eprints.qut.edu.au.

Howker, E., & Malik, S. (2013). *Jilted generation: How Britain has bankrupted its youth*. London, UK: Icon Books Ltd.

Huws, U. (2007). *The spark in the engine: Creative work in the new economy*. London, UK: The Merlin Press Ltd.

Ito, M., Guitiérrez, K., Livingstone, S., Penuel, B., Rhodes, J., Salen, K., . . . Watkins, S. C. (2013). *Connected learning: An agenda for research and design*. Irvine, CA: Digital Media and Learning Research Hub. Retrieved from http://dmlhub.net/publications/connected-learning-agenda-research-and-design

Jones, J., & Schmitt, J. (2014). *A college degree is no guarantee*. Washington, DC: Center for Economic and Policy Research.

Kennedy, H. (2011). *Net work*. London, UK: Palgrave.

Kirshner, B. (2015). *Youth activism in an era of education inequality*. New York, NY: NYU Press.

Krytyka Polityczna, & European Cultural Foundation (Eds.). (2015). *Build the city: Perspectives on commons and culture*. Amsterdam: European Cultural Foundation.

Lally, V., & Doyle, L. (2012). Researching transitions in learning and education: International perspectives on complex challenges and imaginative solutions. *Research in Comparative International Education, 7*(4), 394–408.

Levy, F., & Murnane, R. J. (2004). *The new division of labor: How computers are creating the next job market*. Princeton, NJ: Princeton University Press.

Livermore, O. R. (2013). *The academic grind: A critique of creative and collaborative discourses between digital games industries and postsecondary education in Canada*. Doctoral dissertation, The University of Western Ontario, Ontario.

Lobato, R., Thomas, J., & Hunter, D. (2011). Histories of user-generated content: Between formal and informal media economies. *International Journal of Communication, 5*, 899–914.

Margolis, J., Estrella, R., Goode, J., Holme, J. J., & Nao, K. (2008). *Stuck in the shallow end: Education, race, and computing*. Cambridge, MA: MIT Press.

Mayer, V. (2011). *Below the line: Producers and production studies in the new television economy*. Durham, NC: Duke University Press.

Mayer, V., Banks, M. J., & Caldwell, J. T. (2009). *Production studies: Cultural studies of media industries* (1st ed.). New York, NY: Routledge.

McRobbie, A. (2015). *Be creative: Making a living in the new culture industries*. Cambridge, UK: Polity Press.

Miller, Claire Cain. (2014, May 28). "Google releases employee data, illustrating tech's diversity challenge." *New York Times*. Retrieved from https://bits.blogs.nytimes.com/2014/05/28/google-releases-employee-data-illustrating-techs-diversity-challenge

Miller, N., Henwood, F., & Kennedy, H. (Eds.). (2001). *Cyborg lives: Women's technobiographies*. London, UK: Raw Nerve Books Ltd.

Neff, G. (2012). *Venture labor: Work and the Burden of Risk in Innovative Industries*. Cambridge, MA: MIT Press.

Neff, G., Wissinger, E., & Zukin, S. (2005). Entrepreneurial labour among cultural producers: "Cool" jobs in "hot" industries. *Social Semiotics, 15*(3), 3017–3334.

Nelligan, P. (2015). No guarantees: Preparing for long-term precarious employment in the Australian film and television industry. *Social Alternatives, 34*(4), 22–27.

Nixon, S. (2003). *Advertising cultures: Gender, commerce, creativity.* London, UK: Sage Publications Ltd.

Oakley, K. (2009). 'Art works'—*cultural labour markets: A literature review.* London, UK: Creativity, Culture and Education.

Oakley, K., & O'Brien, D. (2016). Learning to labour unequally: Understanding the relationship between cultural production, cultural consumption and inequality. *Social Identities, 22*(5), 1–16.

Petrie, D. (2012). Creative industries and skills: Film education and training in the era of new labour. *Journal of British Cinema and Television, 9*(3), 357–376.

Poyntz, S. R., Coles, R., Fitzsimmons-Frey, H., Bains, A., Sefton-Green, J., & Hoechsmann, M. (2019). The non-formal arts learning sector, youth provision, and paradox in the learning city. *Oxford Review of Education, 45*(2), 258–278. https://doi.org/10.1080/03054985.2018.1551196

Ravenelle, A. J. (2019). *Hustle and gig: Struggling and surviving in the gig economy.* Berkeley, CA: University of California Press.

Rifkin, J. (2001). *Age of access: The new culture of hypercapitalism, where all of life is a paid-for experience.* New York, NY: Jeremy P Tarcher/Putnam.

Saha, A. (2017). *Race and the cultural industries.* Cambridge, UK: Polity Press.

Saxenian, A. (2006). *The new Argonauts: Regional advantage in a global economy.* Cambridge, MA: Harvard University Press.

Sefton-Green, J. (2013). *Learning at not-school: A review of study, theory, and advocacy for education in non-formal settings.* Cambridge, MA: MIT Press.

Sefton-Green, J., & Brown, L. (2014). Mapping learner progression into digital creativity: Catalysts & disconnects. *State of the Art Review.* Retrieved from www.nominettrust.org.uk/sites/default/files/Mapping%20learner%20progression%20into%20digital%20creativity%20FINAL.pdf

Selingo, J. (2013). *College (un)bound: The future of higher education and what it means for students.* New York, NY: Houghton Mifflin Harcourt Publishing.

Sennett, R. (2007). *The culture of the new capitalism.* New Haven, CT: Yale University Press.

Sennett, R., & Cobb, J. (1973). *The hidden injuries of class.* New York, NY: Vintage.

Soep, L., & Chávez, V. (2010). *Drop that knowledge: Youth radio stories.* Berkeley, CA: University of California Press.

Sperlich, R. (2011). The mixed blessing of autonomy in digital cultural production: A study on filmmaking, press photography and architecture in Austria. *European Journal of Communication, 26*(2), 133–146.

Srnicek, N., & Williams, A. (2016). *Inventing the future: Postcapitalism and a world without work* (Revised, updated ed.). London, UK: Verso.

Standing, G. (2016). *The precariat: The new dangerous class* (Bloomsbury Revelations ed.). London, UK: Bloomsbury Academic.

Stevens, R., O'Connor, K., Garrison, L., Jocuns, A., & Amos, D. M. (2008). Becoming an engineer: Toward a three dimensional view of engineering learning. *Journal of Engineering Education, 97*(3), 355–368.

Taylor, P., Fry, R., & Oates, R. (2014). *The rising cost of not going to college.* Washington, DC: Pew Research Center.

Taylor, S., & Littleton, K. (2008a). Art work or money: Conflicts in the construction of a creative identity. *The Sociological Review, 56*(2), 275–292.

Taylor, S., & Littleton, K. (2008b). *Creative careers and non-traditional trajectories*. London, UK: National Arts Learning Network.

Taylor, S., & Littleton, K. (2016). *Contemporary identities of creativity and creative work*. London, UK: Routledge.

Terranova, T. (2004). *Network culture: Politics for the information age*. London, UK: Pluto Press.

Thornton, S. (1995). *Club cultures: Music, media and subcultural capital*. Cambridge, UK: Polity.

Thornton, S. (2009). *Seven days in the art world*. Cambridge, UK: Granta Books.

Threadgold, S. (2017). *Youth, class and everyday struggles* (1st ed.). New York, NY: Routledge.

Tomlinson, M. (2013). *Education, work and identity: Themes and perspectives*. London, UK: Bloomsbury Academic.

Watkins, S. C. (2019). *Don't knock the hustle*. Boston, MA: Beacon Press.

Watkins, S. C., Cho, A., Lomban-Bermudez, A., Shaw, V., Vickery, J., & Weinzimmer, L. (2018). *The digital edge: The evolving world of social, educational and digital inequality*. New York, NY: New York University Press.

2 Being Indie

The DIY Ethos and Indie Game Development

S. Craig Watkins and Andres Lombana-Bermudez

In this chapter and the next, we offer some perspective on young people's journeys into creative work based on fieldwork that extended over a four-year period. The pursuit of creative careers requires many young people to travel pathways that are non-conventional and entrepreneurial. In years past, education—especially a postsecondary credential—was an almost certain path to employment and economic mobility. And while education continues to be important, it is no longer a guarantee to secure and meaningful employment. As a result, young people are increasingly developing an entrepreneurial ethos. In many instances, the entrepreneurial ethic is not necessarily about making money but rather making opportunity.

Our fieldwork took us into a variety of spaces, communities, and ecosystems designed to open up new opportunities for young workers. No matter where the fieldwork took us, the challenges were strikingly similar. Young people, faced with limited employment opportunities, sought to create their own opportunities. This, of course, is easier said than done. A key aspect of our fieldwork was to better understand how young people connect their interests in a creative career—their aspirations—to tangible work—an opportunity. Along the way, we discovered what elsewhere S. Craig Watkins (2019) calls the making of a 'new innovation economy.'

According to Watkins, the new innovation economy expands who we think of as innovators. Whereas innovation in the more conventional paradigm—think Silicon Valley—is overwhelmingly white and male, the new innovation economy is made up of African Americans and women, for example. Further, the new innovation economy expands what is defined as innovation. If Silicon Valley is premised on creating enterprises that make money, the new innovation economy is premised on creating enterprises that, among other things, make a social impact.

In this chapter and the next, we discuss some of the findings from our fieldwork in greater detail. Among other places, we conducted fieldwork in coworking spaces, event venues, hackathons, meet-ups, and small apartments that were used to launch small enterprises. More specifically, this chapter considers the rise of an independent game development collective, Juegos Rancheros. This was essentially an informal organisation of young people who had either worked in the game industry or had aspirations to create games. The innovation ecosystem that they created and the independent games that they developed are sharply distinct from the games made by the triple-A studios. In the next chapter, we shift our attention to a group of young, aspiring music artists looking to leverage their expertise in hip-hop into a career making and performing music. Musicians have a long history of participating in their very own gig economy. While these two innovation ecosystems are different in some notable ways—the indie game collective was predominantly white, while the hip-hop collective was racially and ethnically diverse—they both laboured diligently and creatively to mobilise distinct forms of social, technological, and human capital to pursue their creative and entrepreneurial aspirations. We believe the two cases offer some unique insights into the challenges young people face in their journey to creative work. Further, the case studies illustrate the distinct forms of agency young people practice in pursuing creative careers.

A growing body of research seeks to understand the new forms of labour that many young people are engaged in, including work that is tech-oriented, creative and entrepreneurial. Scholars have variously described this work as 'venture labour' (Neff, 2012), 'hope labour' (Kuehn & Corrigan, 2013), and 'aspirational labour' (Duffy, 2017). The bulk of this literature focuses on the entrepreneurial and economic ambitions that characterise this activity. To be sure, young people labouring to find their own journey into creative work are driven by economic motivations. But our research suggests that they are driven by non-economic motivations too. Thus, the pursuit of a creative career is also influenced by the desire to secure forms of labour that are fulfilling and more meaningful. Faced with a labour market that is heavily stratified and limited in terms of upward mobility, many young people desire creative work not simply to pursue money but to pursue opportunity and dignity too (Watkins, 2019).

Design of the Research

This chapter and the next chapter are based on roughly four years of ethnographic research. More specifically, the research was designed to explore how young people navigate a rapidly evolving economy marked by, among other things, technological transformation, the rise of gig labour, and economic precarity as outlined in the previous chapter. Our fieldwork involved in-depth interviews, participant observations, and the collection of a variety of artefacts that added depth to our analysis. For example, the in-depth interviews allowed us to probe a wide range of young people about their work experiences and creative ambitions. The in-depth interviews also allowed our research team to engage in a deep probing of specific forms of human behaviour and social organisation.

The interviews were framed via the development of a series of protocols that were designed to generate data and insight. All of the in-depth interviews were configured to work as semi-structured conversations (Rubin & Rubin, 2005).

Moreover, ongoing participant observations allowed us to spend extensive time immersed in the many settings that were the terrain for creative work and the side hustle lifestyle that are prominent features of young people's journeys into creative work (Watkins, 2019). As part of our fieldwork, we conducted extensive participant observation with a variety of creative communities, including Juegos Rancheros, a boutique school for interaction design, a cluster of designers, a community of hip-hop artists, and tech-oriented designers and entrepreneurs working in a coworking space. We were able to observe various events, interactions, and activities that both shaped and sharpened our analysis. Through deep and persistent engagement, we were able to formulate insights about the social and behavioural dynamics that shape the different settings and ecosystems that were included in our sample. The opportunity to observe young people in action provided a pivotal lens into the world they are building. It is a world that is both an inventive response to precarity and a vivid repudiation of the claims that young people are lazy, entitled, and most, notably, antisocial.

Our researchers also collected artefacts that offer further insight into the people and communities that we studied. While this chapter focuses on independent game developers and artists associated with the design of games, the next chapter focuses on hip-hop artists, including musicians, beat makers, and graphic artists. The collection of artefacts included things like posters, flyers, games, prototypes, CDs, websites, social media, videos, promotional materials, press clippings, and internal communication that offer additional perspective on the many different practices young people deploy along the journey to creative work.

Rethinking the Innovation Economy

The transition from an industrial economy to a knowledge economy has been the subject of extensive exploration. Richard Florida's (2002) work on the rising influence of the 'creative economy' and the 'creative class' points to the formation of whole new industries and modes of work. The development of what Enrico Moretti (2012) calls 'innovation hubs' refers to the formation of innovative enterprises and the educated and highly skilled talent they recruit. Researchers have also highlighted the formation of 'innovation districts' (Katz & Wagner, 2014). These are small enclaves of entrepreneurial activity that support innovative enterprises across a variety of sectors—tech, energy, health—with the expressed purpose of catalysing economic development. Erik Brynjolfsson and Andrew McAfee (2014) examine the 'second machine age,' a period characterised by rapid computerisation and automation. This literature, more broadly, points to what we might call the formal innovation economy.

Wealthy tech companies, downtown-based innovation hubs, and elite universities power the formal innovation economy. These entities have access to enormous sums of economic, social, and human capital. In places like Silicon Valley, Seattle, Boston, and New York, the convergence of these resources make up the modern-day version of what sociologist C. Wright Mills (1956) called the 'power elite.' In this iteration of the power elite, access to financial and human capital is restricted to a select few rather than the capable many.

Most young people, needless to say, do not have access to the innovation labs created by companies like Google and Apple, vibrant downtown tech hubs funded by venture capital, or the classrooms and laboratories available to university faculty and students. But this has not prohibited young people from pursuing their own notions of innovation. In our case studies, we shift the gaze to more improvisational modes of innovation. The young people, activities, and spaces that we tracked reside largely on the margins of the formal innovation economy. In this context, young people's journeys to creative work are marked by alternative practices, modes of resource mobilisation, and physical spaces that facilitate new forms of innovation in media, tech, design, and civic life.

This chapter and the next are guided by a set of core questions that structured our fieldwork. These questions included, for example, how does economic precarity influence the decisions young people make regarding their careers? What challenges do young people face in their pursuit of creative careers? What kinds of assets do young people cultivate to pursue creative careers? Two assets that proved to be crucial in our case studies were technology and social capital. As we note in both case studies, technology is important for many reasons, including the degree to which it lowers the barrier to entry by making entrepreneurship more affordable and therefore accessible. The inventive use of software, for example, supports the creation of professional quality media even when young game developers and music makers had very few financial resources.

Contrary to popular opinion, young people's creative practices are not strictly digital. In fact, their pursuit of economic opportunity is remarkably social. Our case studies suggest that young people consistently seek out ways to grow their social capital. In fact, by cultivating more diverse social networks young people enhance their access to rich sources of information, knowledge, and talent.

The literature on 'creative economies' and 'innovation districts' typically overlooks the disparities that are central features of the innovation economy. For example, how do the social dynamics related to race and ethnicity or class and income inequality structure access to and participation in the innovation economy? Thus, a key aspect of our fieldwork was to consider how young people strive to work around these disparities as they labour to secure more creative forms of employment. The cases that we present are not celebratory. Instead, they underscore the significant challenges young people face along their journeys to creative work. Many of the young people we met struggled to cobble together the resources to power their own innovation ecosystems in the context of precarious labour and economic uncertainty.

White-Collar Sweatshops: Work in the Game Industry

Between 2005 and 2009, the game industry in Austin, Texas, flourished. Many of the major companies, including Disney, Electronic Arts, and Blizzard, set up satellite studios in town. But massive technological, behavioural, and industrial change was on the horizon. For example, technological change was reflected in the rise of online and smartphone-enabled gaming. Behavioural changes can be observed in how people play games, including casually and primarily via a handheld. These technological and behavioural changes have compelled the industry to devise new strategies regarding the games they produce and the marketplace they serve.

The currents of change precipitated reorganisation in the game industry. Many of the satellite studios in Austin, for example, began cutting back their financial commitment, laying off workers, or closing their doors. During this period. the changes were a response, in part, to console games' loss of market share and cultural status to social, mobile, and massive online gaming platforms. These and other shifts in the industry apply even more pressure than usual in an industry that has long been vulnerable to social, financial, and technological flux. As the US Bureau of Labor Statistics (Liming & Vilorio, 2011, p. 10) reports, a bad game or one with low sales 'could mean financial trouble for a studio and its employees.'

In addition to these broad structural forces that undermine work in the industry, the workplace culture in game studios is undergoing increasing scrutiny. In recent years, the wider tech industry has faced serious criticism for its lack of workforce diversity and unscrupulous business tactics. The game industry is no exception. Many of the indie game developers we met shared a variety of concerns about the workplace culture common in triple-A studios. Take, for instance, the practice of 'crunch.' Former studio employees noted how the practice leads to stress and sweatshop-like conditions.

Crunch is an industry term used to describe the frequent demand that employers place on their employees to work an excessive number of hours, as many as 70 to 80 a week, to deliver a game on time. In a 2017 study of game developers conducted by International Game Developer Association more than half, 51 percent, of the respondents reported that their studios practiced crunch (Weststar, O'Meara, & Legault, 2017).

Juegos members also expressed trepidation about the fickle nature of work in the game industry. Many of them liked the idea of making games but lamented the fact that work in the studios is often perilous. Most of the young people we met who worked in the industry were typically hired as contract workers. The game industry is notorious for cyclical employment driven by periods of high demand for labour on the one hand and periods of low demand on the other. Work in the industry for many is a form of gig labour. The 2017 International Games Developers Association report found that the average game industry employee changes jobs every 2.4 years. It also explained that permanent employees 'are often hired and let go.' Their job security, it turns out, is not much better than those who work in the industry as freelancers.

We frequently heard complaints that working in a corporate studio also meant signing non-disclosure agreements or NDAs. These legally binding agreements meant that studio employees could not discuss the games that they were working on with people outside their studio. Many were also asked to sign non-compete clauses, which meant that they could not make their own games. More than a few Juegos members described these conditions as imprisoning. A number of game developers and artists had aspirations to make their own games—a creative goal that was not permissible as a result of working for a corporate studio.

One of the benefits for Juegos's members who formerly worked in the game industry was the opportunity to be in a community that invited them to talk about their projects, share ideas, and engage in what researchers call 'open innovation' (Chesbrough, 2003; Watkins, 2019). Whereas the corporate studio model requires secrecy and a silo mentality, the open innovation model encourages the exchange of ideas, the sharing of expertise, and collaboration across disciplines and organisations.

Trends like these—crunch, contract-based employment, corporate-imposed restrictions—create working conditions that are unhealthy, unstable, and uninspiring. The game industry, like the knowledge economy more generally, represents what Jill Andresky Fraser (2001) calls 'white-collar sweatshops.' These types of conditions underscore the broader trends that render work in the knowledge economy precarious and unglamorous, despite the celebratory tone common in the press and the corporate sector.

The Making of an Indie Game Collective

The creation of Juegos Rancheros, an indie game collective based in Austin, Texas, offers a revealing look into how aspiring game developers responded to the reorganisation of the local game industry. The group consisted of game developers, artists, writers, designers, and filmmakers. Juegos's founders realised a need for some kind of collective activity in the wake of the widespread studio retrenchment and shutdowns that pushed a number of people out of the game development industry. Faced with a reduced industry footprint in Austin and uneven demand for tech workers, the founders of the collective sensed an opportunity to build an independent game development ecosystem. Before Juegos, there was no organised mechanism for the displaced workers and growing community of young designers, developers, artists, and media creators to meet regularly, network, share ideas, and catalyse indie game development. The Juegos Rancheros collective was a creative solution.

In this chapter, we highlight two specific aspects of the Juegos indie game collective. First, we explore how this particular group of indie game developers leveraged technology to forge open new spaces for innovation and game creation. Second, we explain how the collective also maneuvered to grow its social capital by creating several opportunities to make connections that expanded their access to the resources pivotal in the pursuit of creative work like knowledge, support, and talent. The tech and social ingenuity demonstrated by Juegos illuminates how young people navigate structural constraints and economic precarity to fashion their own innovation economy.

Tech and the DIY Ethos

Several of the game developers and artists who participated in the Juegos collective worked in what they called 'micro-studios.' These were usually modest enterprises that consisted of two to three members. Additionally, micro-studios were set in a variety of spaces, including small apartments, coffee shops, and the virtual world of the Internet. Meetings occurred face-to-face, via video conferencing, and through software like Slack that allows teams to work together in a distributed and asynchronous fashion. Micro-studios do not have the financial and human capital that is commonly available in the triple-A studios. Consequently, the young developers we met in the Juegos collective adopted the do-it-yourself (DIY) ethos to make their games.

One of the most significant shifts in media culture over the last 40 years is the rise of DIY media production. There is, in fact, a long legacy of DIY media production in film, print, and music. A critical factor in DIY media is the ability of technology to open up space for a greater diversity of media producers by lowering the barrier to entry. In film, for example, the availability of affordable high-end cameras to make professional-quality films opened up space for new storytellers. In print, the spread of typewriters and later word processing software democratised the production of high-quality print media. The rise of multi-track and advanced audio equipment has enlivened indie music production.

Technology also enhances DIY media production by opening up new distribution channels. For example, a growing roster of film festivals and the Internet expand the venues to distribute independent films.

Developments like the Xerox machine made it easy to reproduce and circulate print media. The Internet accelerates the distribution of new modes of print media in the form of interest-driven blogs, newsletters, and other online publications. Similarly, the capacity to distribute music via cassette tapes, CDs, and the Internet has unleashed successive generations of indie music artists. Technological developments like these have also lowered the barrier to producing interactive forms of media like games.

Tech Ingenuity and Indie Game Development

The emergence of cheap tools in digital arts, design, and, interactive media have forged open new frontiers for indie game developers to make games with impressive graphics and challenging gameplay mechanics. The technology to produce indie games—especially professional quality three-dimensional games—is a relatively recent phenomenon. Whereas the triple-A studios continue to assert substantial influence in the production of games, their dominance is not nearly as absolute as it once was due, in part, to technological advances.

In our conversations with indie game developers, we heard about a wide mix of software that was adopted to support indie game creation. A few Juegos members told us about Gimp, a free alternative to Photoshop. Gimp is an open-source graphics editor that can be used for image retouching, editing, and free-form drawing. We also learned about Silo, described by one indie game developer as an inexpensive 3D modelling program. Another artist used Blender, a free software, to do animation. For sound design, many Juegos members used open access or cheap tools like freesound.org and Apple's Garage Band. One game developer mentioned that he's worked on projects that used Audacity, a free and open-source digital audio editor and recording application software.

YouTube has also emerged as a powerful asset in the innovation economy created by indie game developers. Similar to their counterparts in music, television, and film, many indie game developers use YouTube to promote and build a community around their content. YouTube has become a significant asset in gaming culture. Many of the channel's top 'influencers' and most subscribed to channels come from the gaming sector. Juegos's members used YouTube to help build the identity and presence of their micro-studios in the larger indie game developer economy. Among other things, the indie developers used YouTube to release gameplay sequences of their games, commentary, and trailers through their carefully crafted YouTube channels. In this context, YouTube was a resource for sharing content, storytelling, brand recognition, and community building.

The most significant tech breakthrough for indie game developers is the widely used game engine, Unity. According to most of the young developers we interviewed, Unity is the standard, the tool that allows indie game developers to affordably produce high-quality games in terms of graphics and gameplay mechanics. Unity was officially released in July 2005. The goal was clear and ambitious. 'We have always wanted to change the way the game industry looks today where it requires a ridiculous amount of money to make PC and Mac games,' said Unity co-founder and CEO at the time, David Helgason, in the press release announcing the new engine (Carless, 2005a).

Today, more games are made with Unity than with any other platform in the world. Unity has helped to produce games across multiple platforms, including PCs, consoles, mobile, virtual reality, and the web. Experiences made with Unity reach more than three billion devices worldwide, according to Unity. The game creation platform was especially popular among members of the Juegos collective. 'Unity is a game engine, it's what basically drives the game,' one member of Juegos told us. 'It's where you put all your art; it's where you put all your code, and you put it together into a game there,' he explained. His partner, added, 'Unity is like Microsoft Word for creating games.' 'It's your editor,' he continued. 'You build everything inside of it, and it gives you all the tools for doing that.'

In addition to a new generation of tools and software that have lowered the barrier to producing games, a number of platforms lowered the barrier to distributing games. Several members of the Juegos collective, for example, used itch.io to distribute their games. Founded in 2013, itch.io is an open marketplace that offers indie game developers a chance to sell the games that they make. All transactions on itch.io are 'pay-what-you-want pricing.' There are different pricing levels within this model. In some cases, an indie game developer might ask a potential consumer to simply donate an amount they believe is appropriate for their game. In other cases, the developer might establish a fixed price for the game. Itch.io also offers developers analytics related to how people discover and play their games, adding another dimension in the evolution of indie game development.

Several indie game developers that we met took advantage of the long-tail economy made possible via the Internet (Anderson, 2006). Whether it is the burgeoning mobile app economy or web-based platforms, indie game developers have far more opportunities to cultivate a market for their games. And while these distribution channels are modest compared to the channels available to the corporate studios, they do establish access to niche tastes, gamers, and the opportunity to generate both financial and reputational capital.

These technological breakthroughs forged open space for different interpretations of what games could be. The makers of Unity anticipated the disruption that was coming to the gaming world. More specifically, they saw the arrival of a new generation of game developers who were not tied to the corporate studios. 'What the casual revolution needs most is not huge art teams, but creative individuals with clever, different, wacky ideas,' said one Unity executive (Carless, 2005b). We certainly saw evidence of this—different ideas—in the Juegos collective. Many of the indie game developers from Juegos gravitated towards the build of games that were unconventional in terms of genre, art, and story. As one Juegos participant told us, 'we want to make games that get away from white dudes wearing headsets and screaming insults at each other.'

Members of the Juegos collective approached game development as an opportunity to make games that were personal, expressive, and idiosyncratic. For example, Juegos developers made games that challenged the male gaze common in the industry, the propensity for violence, and the preference for commerce and action over art and storytelling (Watkins, 2019).

Game Jamming

Several members of the Juegos collective credit another interesting tech-enabled practice for their innovative approach to game development: game jams. An indie game designer we met described this particular invention as follows:

> Game jams are similar to hackathons and usually involve a challenge that involves making a playable game in a finite amount of time, usually about forty-eight hours. Some game jams are held online while others happen offline.

The last game jam that this Juegos member participated in was held in an abandoned yoga studio. 'It was empty, and they just filled it with tables, power strips, network cables, pizza, beer, bottled water, and everybody just went there.' The game jam took place over a three-day period. 'You had to complete your game within that time. And so it was just, like, an around-the-clock everybody working on their games.' Some of the participants brought desktop computers, fully loaded laptops, and other equipment to set up what were essentially mobile studios.

Game jams bring people with different expertise together to produce a solution to a specific problem in a finite amount of time. The core idea is to connect participants with different skill sets—animators, programmers, writers—to build games quickly and in a spirit of collaboration and experimentation. A game jam may be organised to develop games that address a specific challenge—for example, in the civic or education space. In other instances, the game jam may experiment with a new gameplay mechanic, design technique, or piece of software. The main point is to generate an idea for a game and build it fast. In the world of design, this is known as *rapid prototyping*.

Technology and design companies regularly use rapid prototyping to accelerate ideation, experimentation, and innovation. Rapid prototypes are usually not polished or finished. In fact, rapid prototypes are intentionally cheap, fast, and iterative. It is precisely these attributes—fast, cheap, and iterative—that make the practice a perfect complement for indie developers, artists, and makers who have few financial or institutional resources at their disposal. Kyle, an Austin-based indie game developer, appreciated game jams for their capacity to catalyse rapid prototyping. 'The one thing that I've learned from Juegos is the best way to make games is to do fast prototyping,' Kyle told us.

> That's why game jams are such a big thing. Like, so many games come from game jams because people are forced to not sit and bellyache over every little detail; they have forty-eight hours to just get something done. And because they're restricted in what they can do, they do it, and they actually finish a game. And that can be the seed for a bigger game.

Several other indie game developers echoed Kyle's thoughts. There is a long list of reasons why an aspiring developer may never actually make a playable game. Obviously, the lack of financial resources is a huge hurdle. So is the lack of personnel or the studio space to build a fully playable game. But game jams are designed to work around these and other obstacles by imposing strict time and technical constraints. There is no expectation that you will make a ready to go to market game, but rather that you can build something that expresses an idea, a technical feature, distinct gameplay experience, or a proof of concept. Game jams are designed to spark innovation, not perfection.

The more we listened to Juegos developers talk about game jams, the more we came to understand how this clever use of technology and human capital strengthened indie game development. Some of the developers we met treated game jams like an innovation lab or a space to experiment with new ideas, skills, or technology. A noted feature of the economy that young people have inherited is the responsibility they must assume for maintaining their skills and employability. Some researchers call this new reality the 'risk economy,' a reference to the fact that a rising share of workers today bear the responsibility for maintaining and upgrading their skills for an ever-evolving labour market (Hacker, 2006). A key feature of young people's journeys into creative work is figuring out ways to grow their human capital.

Because the technology used to produce interactive media evolves so quickly, indie game developers have to figure out ways to stay up-to-date with new software and the implications for content creation. This explains, in part, why some indie game makers use game jams as a laboratory to test new ideas, skills, or technologies. Lacking access to a studio, regular work colleagues, or formal professional development opportunities, many game designers have gravitated towards informal spaces and activities like game jams to keep their media-making skills crisp.

One game developer noted, 'Game jams are a fun way to keep your ideas fresh.' The most recent game jam that he and some of his colleagues participated in 'was a way to try something different and just completely change directions and exercise some creativity,' he said. He continued,

> Game jams are just a good way to perfect your skills, but for me, it's also just to try out an idea. Oftentimes you'll think of an idea and be, like, 'I really want to try this sometime,' but you just never come around to it. I've been wanting to make a zero-gravity game for a long time, and the game jam kind of coincided, so we decided to do that.

Jonathan agreed that game jams were a great excuse to try things one ordinarily might not.

> Yes, it is a great excuse for that because even though you may be way out of your comfort zone, it's a great excuse to put yourself out there. So in this case it's, like, 'Well, why not?' If it fails, the only risk is that you lost a weekend or something like that, but you probably learned something.

Finally, Juegos's use of game jams achieved another purpose. The co-founders of the indie game development collective recognised that the studio layoffs left a number of people unemployed and isolated from each other. Juegos was constantly seeking out ways—meet-ups, design boot camps, workshops, game jams—for indie game developers to maintain a sense of identity and community. The game jams exposed members to other indie game developers and creative types across Austin, the US, and the world. Exposure to a greater diversity of ideas about games, design, and storytelling influences how game developers approach their craft. In short, the game jams were not simply an opportunity to make games; they were also an opportunity to make connections that generated important social and creative benefits.

A Social Capital Hub

The members of the Juegos collective were not only savvy in terms of how they manoeuvred to use technology. They were also savvy in terms of how they manoeuvred to use social networks. One of the most significant features of the Juegos collective was the degree to which it fostered the cultivation of social capital.

During our fieldwork, we learned that there was a significant number of developers and artists who pursued indie game creation. The efforts to fashion their own game development ecosystem reflect the broader trend towards self-employment and 'gig labour' in the wider economy. In the US, the percentage of people working in what the National Bureau of

Economic Research calls, 'alternative work' is growing (Katz & Krueger, 2016). This is a reference to the individuals who are self-employed or who work, for example, as freelancers, gig workers, and independent contractors.

In 2005, 11 percent of workers were involved in alternative work arrangements (Katz & Krueger, 2016). By 2015, that figure rose to 16 percent. Virtually all of the young former employees in the game industry took up alternative work arrangements to pursue game development. Some of them held jobs in the tech sector (usually non-prestige jobs in customer service, testing, or clerical), while many others worked in service sector employment. The micro-studios relied on itinerant staff to make their games. In these instances, individuals worked on games in small teams, sometimes without pay, and asynchronously. Working conditions like these can lead to a sense of social isolation, a condition that the founders of the Juegos collective were keenly aware of. Juegos's signature event—a monthly meet-up—was designed to address the degree to which young game developers lacked opportunities to build their social connections. This event provided a regular opportunity for indie game developers to grow their social ties, social networks, and, as a result, access to the resources necessary to realise their creative and entrepreneurial ambitions.

The Juegos monthly meet-up often featured a set of planned activities, such as a demo of a game, a presentation, and announcements. However, the most significant portion of the event was the opportunity for attendees to simply hang out and meet each other. This feature allowed attendees to catch up with old acquaintances and make new ones. The face-to-face interactions were a chance to get up-to-date information about what was happening in this community of developers, designers, and artists. This was the time when attendees could learn about a new project someone was working on, how a crowdfunding project was doing, or that a studio in town was looking for talent. A person who is proficient at coding for mobile applications might learn through an informal conversation that the developer of a new mobile game was looking for a programmer to help shore up the technical features of his or her game. A founder of a micro-studio in search of a character artist might be introduced to artists during a meet-up. Small talk like this was typical during the meet-ups and occasionally led to an opportunity to find work, a chance for collaboration, or inspiration.

It turns out that small talk, gossip, and rumours actually perform a valuable social function in ecosystems like Juegos (Dunbar, 1997). The circulation of information such as who is looking for talent is crucial to sustaining a vibrant social network. Previous research strongly suggests that access to information channels like this is key to occupational mobility. It is often assumed that people are hired strictly on merit but research suggests, 'who we know' is just as crucial as 'what we know'

(Granovetter, 1995). The monthly meet-up established a ready-made environment for attendees to expand who they knew in this eclectic community of creative types.

The casual conversations and the surprising bits of information that they circulated were some of the features of the meet-up that participants enjoyed. 'I mean the whole idea [of the meet-up] is you come, and you have a beer, and you start a conversation with someone who knows something that you don't,' one indie game developer told us. 'And it might not even have anything to do with games, but it could help your game or help turn you on to a game that you hadn't heard of before.'

Natalie noted the meet-up was just as much about making social connections as it was making games. 'For me, the most important thing about this event is not even the games but the people who are here to see the games making those connections, shaking the hands of people, trading business cards.' During a meet-up, Natalie elaborated, 'No one here is an industry hotshot. We're all just doing something out of passion and excitement. It's really exciting to sort of forge those community networks.' Kevin appreciated the subtle nuances that made the meet-up a regular event on his social calendar.

> My favorite part of Juegos is just the energy here. Like it's obviously this really great supportive community of people who really get behind each other and root for each other, but also support each other's games with new ideas, and introducing them to other people and stuff.

This was the real purpose of Juegos in general and the meet-up specifically. That is, to create a space for indie game developers to connect with each other, explore game creation with each other, and, when the opportunity presented itself, build games and a distinct innovation ecosystem with each other.

The Pop-Up Economy: Reimagining the Video Arcade

During our fieldwork, we observed the design of 'pop-up arcades.' The pop-up model is a notable feature of the new innovation economy (Watkins, 2019). Pop-up models are temporary physical spaces in retail and consumer goods that can be set up, removed, and relocated with relative ease. As the concept continues to evolve, pop-up shops have been used in a variety of sectors, including tech, food, fashion, media, and art. The pop-up arcade is a space where a public of creative workers and video game consumers come together to experience a distinct culture of indie gaming in a temporary physical space.

The pop-up concept is ideal for young entrepreneurs like the members of the Juegos collective for a variety of reasons. For instance, the pop-up model allows aspiring entrepreneurs to launch an idea in a low-cost, low-risk physical environment. Equally important, entrepreneurs are able to assess the viability of their idea in the real world. The pop-up arcade is a unique iteration of the video arcade, a particular kind of public amusement space that became popular among US youth in the 1970s and 1980s (Kocurek, 2012; June 2013). The pop-up arcade parallels the broader new innovation economy that many aspirational artists and innovators participate in. This economy is iterative, flexible, and predicated on tech and social ingenuity (Watkins, 2019).

With deeper roots in the history of American popular culture that go back to the amusement parlours of the 19th century and the nickelodeons and pinball arcades of the 20th century, the video arcade is part of a long tradition of spaces for play, social life, and interaction with media technologies (June 2013). For more than a century, the arcade, as a public space for showcasing and playing media novelties (e.g. phonographs, kinetoscopes, electro-mechanical games, video games) has continually been reimagined and repurposed. In its various iterations, the arcade has been a site for the development of a range of practices that reflect the characteristics of particular social, cultural, economic, and technological contexts.

The glowing video screens, custom-built cabinets, coins, action games, and youth (especially males), characterised the Golden Age arcade of the 1970s and 1980s. Embracing the values of the commercial marketplace, this space became a major driver of not only the commodification of video games but also the masculinisation of video game culture (Kocurek, 2012). Pay-for-play practices were encouraged at the arcade by an emergent video game industry influenced by manufacturers, distributors, operators, and arcade owners who were interested in maximising profits. Although arcade visitors could simply hang out, watch others play, or enjoy the screens showing demos of the games, most attendees spent their money on playing games (Kocurek, 2012).

Indie game communities like Juegos Rancheros are reimagining the video arcade by making a version that is based on values that vary substantially from the values embraced in the Golden Age era. If the arcades in the 1970s and 1980s were predominantly built for teen boys and young men, then the pop-up arcades designed by Juegos invite all types of gamers—males and females, young people and their older counterparts. In the Golden Age arcade, the game titles were dominated by fighting, action, and shooter games. By contrast, games in the pop-up arcade represent gameplay experiences that are more eclectic and idiosyncratic. The games that were featured in the pop-up arcades were usually independently produced or curated from game jams sponsored by Juegos.

We also began to think about the pop-up arcade as a type of 'gift economy.' According to Lewis Hyde (1983), the gift economy is a kind of non-market economy that supports social life. Hyde explains, 'When gifts circulate within a group, their commerce leaves a series of intercon-nected relationships in its wake, and a kind of decentralized cohesiveness emerges' (p. 20). Hence, by circulating gifts in the pop-up arcade, partici-pants of Juegos Rancheros establish social connections with each other that support the maintenance of a community.

For example, participants in the Juegos's pop-up arcades—developers, arcade designers, and attendees—engaged in a range of exchanges that were 'gift' oriented rather than 'market' oriented. For instance, instead of relying on the pay-for-play practice of the Golden Era arcades, the indie games featured in the pop-up arcade are free. Attendees do not need coins or tokens to operate the computers, mobile devices, or custom-built arcade cabinets loaded with indie games. In return, attendees give game developers and pop-up arcade designers feedback and ideas related to the design of their games or pop-up arcades. Developers can observe in real time how well their games—everything from the artwork and audio to the gameplay mechanics—connect with audiences. The arcade designers can also learn from the audience whether the design of the space sparks enthusiasm and appreciation for indie games.

In this gift economy, the pop-up arcade is a source of inspiration and community making rather than commodification and money making. One Juegos participant described having his game featured in a pop-up arcade this way: 'Having your game exhibited at the arcade is like your turn to get in front of your peers and show what you have been working on. You have a unique opportunity to get feedback and engage with an audience.' Another young developer echoed these sentiments.

> The games that are shown here and the people who come, they're not necessarily about making a profit, or making the game that sells the most copies, or makes the most money. And the people are just driven by passion for gaming and passion for the community.

Conclusion

As we explain in this chapter and the next, young people looking to attain careers that are rewarding—personally and financially—are increasingly seeking to build their own pathways to such careers. This represents a degree of creativity and agency that is articulated largely through tech and social ingenuity. For example, they are leveraging a variety of technolo-gies, such as production-oriented software and social media, to establish pathways to creative work. But young people's investment in their future is not strictly about 'being digital.' It is also about being social. They are also showing inventiveness in the creation of events, spaces, and activities that fortify their ability to grow what they know—human capital—and who they know—social capital. Finally, the pursuit of creative work is also an opportunity to assert more agency in their careers and in their lives.

References

Anderson, C. (2006). *The long tail: Why the future of business is selling less of more*. New York: Hyperion.

Brynjolfsson, E., & McAfee, A. (2014). *The second machine age: Work, progress, and prosperity in a time of brilliant technologies*. New York, NY: W. W. Norton.

Carless, S. (2005a, July 14). *OvertheEdge announces Unity 1.0.2. release*. Gamasutra: The art and business of making games. Retrieved from www.gamasutra.com/view/news/96897/OverTheEdge_Announces_Unity_102_Release.php

Carless, S. (2005b, August 23). *OTEE releases Unity 1.1 game engine*. Gamasutra: The art and business of making games. Retrieved from www.gamasutra.com/view/news/97262/OTEE_Releases_Unity_11_Game_Engine.php

Chesbrough, H. (2003). The era of open innovation. *MIT Sloan Management Review*, 44(3), 35–41.

Duffy, B. E. (2017). *(Not) getting paid to do what you love: Gender, social media, and aspirational work*. New Haven, CT: Yale University Press.

Dunbar, R. (1997). *Grooming, gossip, and the evolution of language*. Cambridge, MA: Harvard University Press.

Florida, R. (2002). *The rise of the creative class: And how it's transforming work, leisure, community and everyday life*. New York, NY: Basic Books.

Fraser, J. A. (2001). *White-collar sweatshop: The deterioration of work and its rewards in corporate America*. New York, NY: W&W Norton & Company.

Granovetter, M. (1995). *Getting a job: A study of contacts and careers* (2nd ed.). Chicago, IL: University of Chicago Press.

Hacker, J. S. (2006). *The great risk shift: The assault on American jobs, families, health care, and retirement and how you can fight back*. New York, NY: Oxford University Press.

Hyde, Lewis. *The gift: Imagination and the erotic life of property*. New York, NY: Penguin Random House, 1983.

June, L. (2013, January 16). For amusement only: The life and death of the American arcade. *The Verge*. Retrieved from www.theverge.com/2013/1/16/3740422/the-life-and-death-of-the- american-arcade-for-amusement-only

Katz, L. B., & Krueger, A. B. (2016, September). *The rise and nature of alternative work arrangements in the United States, 1995–2015*. NBER Working Paper No. 22667. National Bureau of Economic Research.

Katz, L. B., & Wagner, J. (2014). *The rise of innovation districts: A new geography of innovation in America*. Metropolitan Policy Program at Brookings. Washington, DC: Brookings Institution.

Kocurek, C. A. (2012). *Masculinity at the video game arcade: 1972–1983*. Doctoral dissertation, American Studies Department, University of Texas, Austin. Retrieved from https://repositories.lib.utexas.edu/handle/2152/22133

Kuehn, K., & Corrigan, F. C. (2013). Hope labor: The role of employment prospects in online social production. *Political Economy of Communication*, 1(1), 9–25.

Liming, D., & Vilorio, D. (2011). Work for play: Careers in video game development. *Occupational Outlook Quarterly*, 55(3), 2–11.

Mills, C. W. (1956). *The power elite*. New York, NY: Oxford University Press.

Moretti, E. (2012). *The new geography of jobs*. New York, NY: Houghton Mifflin Harcourt.

Neff, G. (2012). *Venture labor: Work and the burden of risk in innovative industries*. Cambridge, MA: MIT Press.

Rubin, H. J., & Rubin, I. S. (2005). *Qualitative interviewing: The art of hearing qualitative data* (2nd ed.). Thousand Oaks, CA: Sage Publications.

Watkins, S. C. (2019). *Don't knock the hustle: Young creatives, tech ingenuity, and the making of a new innovation economy*. Boston, MA: Beacon Press.

Weststar, J., O'Meara, V., & Legault, M.-J. (2017, January 8) *Developer satisfaction survey 2017: Summary report*. International Game Developer Association. Retrieved from https://cdn.ymaws.com/www.igda.org/resource/resmgr/2017_DSS_/!IGDA_DSS_2017_SummaryReport.pdf

3 Building a Music Innovation Ecosystem

Creative Labour in Hip-Hop Culture

*Andres Lombana-Bermudez
and S. Craig Watkins*

In the previous chapter, we focused on the rise of a collective of independent game developers, Juegos Rancheros. As part of our fieldwork, as we described in Chapter 2, we also spent considerable time with a hip-hop collective made up primarily of rappers, DJs, and beat makers pursuing their aspirations to make music. The group called itself the Austin Mic Exchange (AMX). Still, there were some noteworthy similarities between the two groups. Similar to the indie game collective, AMX members were extraordinarily inventive when it came to cultivating the forms of capital—human, social, and technological—required to pursue their creative ambitions.

There is, of course, a much longer history of independent music production than independent game development. In addition to the technological shifts that lower the barrier to entry in the music business, the music sector, like the game sector, is undergoing a significant structural shift in terms of the production, distribution, and consumption of content. While the AMX collective focuses mainly on music performance (i.e. rapping) and music production (i.e. beat making), there were instances of entrepreneurs looking to make their mark in design, graphic art, photography, and merchandising. In this chapter, we focus mainly on the rappers, DJs, and beat makers who made up the core members of AMX.

As upstart artists, the members of AMX laboured without the benefits of any formal institutional support provided by music labels or local industry. Still, in this chapter, we argue that this collection of rappers, DJs, and beat makers skilfully leveraged their limited resources to form a distinct innovation ecosystem. AMX functioned simultaneously as a platform, a community, and a laboratory that helped young artists establish on-ramps into the local music industry. As a platform, AMX was a catalyst for helping its members develop the skills that are crucial to finding opportunities in a rapidly evolving music industry. As a community, AMX was an extraordinarily rich social system, providing distinct opportunities for members to offer each other support, material resources, and the sharing of expertise. As a laboratory, AMX functioned much like a learning laboratory for aspiring artists to experiment with new ideas, music, and entrepreneurship.

This collective of hip-hop artists laboured on the margins of the local music industry in Austin, Texas. Over the years, Austin has developed a reputation as the 'live music capital of the world'—a brand that city leaders and music entrepreneurs have worked hard to promote. But hip-hop was clearly marginal in the overall music scene and economy that shaped Austin's local music economy. We spent time in the specific venue that was home to the open mic night organised by the co-founders of AMX as well as the small apartments and bedrooms that served as the studios for music making in this particular ecosystem. We observed showcases, small concert performances, and local productions, like video shoots. We spoke to a mix of artists in AMX to learn more about the challenges they faced and the aspirations they cultivated. This aspect of the music industry—small, independent, online, and offline—reflects the inventive ways music artists pursue their creative and entrepreneurial ambitions in an industry marked by social, technological, and economic transformation.

Our analysis of AMX is situated in the context of the music industry transformation specifically and the increasingly precarious employment and economic circumstances faced by young adults more generally. In this chapter, we consider the inventive practices developed by the AMX collective. Thus, we consider their efforts to cultivate some of the resources that are crucial to building a culture of innovation. More precisely, our analysis centres on the development of key forms of capital, including physical, human, social, and technological.

The New Music Economy

Careers in the music industry, corporate or independent, have always been competitive and challenging. Turning their passion for music into a professional career has never been easy for young aspiring artists. Whereas economic mobility in the music business historically has been contingent on developing a relationship with a corporate label, this model has become less true over the years. Today, breaking into the music industry is difficult not only because the pathways of entry are not straightforward but also because the industry is undergoing structural transformations due, in part, to the disruptions provoked by digital technologies like smartphones, music apps, and music streaming. It has never been easier or harder to start a music career than it is today. Digital tools—music creation software (i.e. GarageBand), laptops serving as mobile studios, video, and music distribution platforms (i.e. YouTube), music apps (i.e. SoundCloud), and social media (i.e. Twitter) make it easier than ever before to create and share music. But these same technologies also mean that just about anyone can create and share music. One of the biggest challenges in today's tech-driven media economy, according to one of our interviewees, is that 'anyone can make media today.' And while this is not entirely true, it does suggest that the increasing democratisation of media production creates unanticipated problems like standing out in what has been described by some as a fiercely competitive 'attention economy.'

The adoption of digital tools has altered professional practices in the music industry related to music production, distribution, and marketing. Music production has been transformed by easier access to recording equipment and software. Changes in music distribution have been accelerated by the spread of peer-to-peer networks and streaming services on the Internet. The ability of musicians to interact directly with fans changes long-standing, industry-led practices related to marketing and fan engagement. As a result of these and other changes, the music industry is in the midst of a paradigm shift (Tschmuck, 2012, 2017; see also Chapter 6).

Additionally, these changes have provoked a power shift in the music business. The major music companies continue to exercise power in the marketplace, but their influence is no longer absolute as a result of a shifting technological and cultural landscape. Consequently, corporate labels do not exercise total control over the production, distribution, and marketing of music. The rise of relatively cheap tech tools allows upstart independent musicians to produce and distribute their own music. Like other cultural products, music is no longer only a physical product (Baym, 2010; Tschmuck, 2012, 2017; Wikström, 2013), which lowers the cost of production significantly. The shift to digital lowers the barrier to entry, in part, by lowering the costs associated with music production, distribution, and marketing.

In our fieldwork, we met several striving hip-hop artists who made music from their bedrooms and small apartments, using relatively affordable tech like laptops and audio software, as well as free tech like social media, to bolster their pursuit of a career in music. In the midst of these shifts, a new music economy based on services, live performances, a mix of gift and commodity exchanges, and music streaming (Baym, 2010; Leyshon, 2014; Wikström, 2013; Watkins, 2019) is forming. Relationships between networked audiences and artists, for instance, have become important not only for developing music careers and fan bases but also for creating new business models. The blueprint for these new models is likely to be designed by artists working on the periphery rather than inside the corporate labels.

As we discuss next, the ever-evolving music economy generates simultaneous risks and opportunities for independent musicians. On the one hand, it opens up new possibilities for experimenting with music production practices and roles that have long been controlled by major companies. In today's rapidly evolving music industry, artists are assuming the roles that used to be played by professionals, such as artist and repertoire development (A&R), marketing, and merchandising. Barriers of entry into the music sector have lowered, and musicians can more easily participate in the production and distribution of music.

But the challenges of operating as an independent persist. For example, competition has increased and an excess supply has emerged in the artistic labour market (Tschmuck, 2017; Towse, 2010). Aspiring musicians do not only need to be good at making music but also at developing skills in marketing, merchandising, managing social media, and maintaining fan communities. (Tschmuck, 2017; Wikström, 2013). These are tasks and roles that require time and expertise, which are both in limited supply for struggling artists armed with few resources. Furthermore, labour is especially precarious. As we have already noted in the introduction to this volume, creative work, under neoliberal capitalism, is characterised by conditions of insecurity, is sporadic and contract based, requires flexibility and mobility, and is often performed without any wage compensation (Frenette, 2013, 2016; Hracs, 2016; Haijen, 2016; De Peuter, 2011; Gill & Pratt, 2008; Neilson & Rossiter, 2005; Pratt, 2000). It has never been easier and harder at the same time to be a musician than it is in the burgeoning digital economy. In fact, many of the artists we observed faced the same dilemma: even as the tools to make and market their music have become more accessible, income-earning opportunities as a creative worker remain elusive.

Along with making a living for themselves, independent musicians also have to make financial investments in equipment and services that help them to move forward in their careers, such as audio gear, post-production studio services, and merchandise manufacturing. According to one aspiring rapper, 'You've got all these extra expenses. Like you actually have to pay to go to the studio, you have to pay for your merchandise that you're going to sell, so you need some type of income coming in.' Most of the artists we met did not earn much income from their creative labour, which limited their ability to make these kinds of financial investments in their careers.

During our fieldwork, we also learned about other financial obstacles that striving artists encounter in their pursuit of a music career. As we discuss next, making it as a music artist requires performing in live shows. It's not only a good way to promote your music. In the increasingly dominant digital music economy, live performance gigs are one of the most reliable ways artists can actually earn income. The music streaming ecosystem is now the future of music distribution and consumption, which is both good news and bad news for independent artists. The good news is that the shift to streaming lowers music production costs. Artists residing on the industry margins can release songs via social media and streaming platforms. The bad news is that even the most popular artists, like Drake and Taylor Swift, make very little income from streaming; see Chapter 6.

Big streaming companies like Spotify and Apple pay roughly $0.006 to $0.0084 per stream to the holder of music rights, which can include labels, publishers, producers, and songwriters (Sehgal, 2018). This suggests that in the music streaming economy, artists are essentially giving away their music for very little in return. Striving artists like the ones who populated AMX make virtually no money from music streaming channels, even though in theory the 'long-tail economy' expands the inventory of music available along the consumer demand curve (Anderson, 2006). Trends like these make live performance—concerts, festivals, and showcases—a major income-earning opportunity.

But access to performance venues and stages can be challenging for unknown artists. A few artists complained to us that they are occasionally asked to pay an appearance cost. The practice, known as 'pay-to-play,' requires artists to pay a fee to live music promoters in order to perform in a showcase or as the opening act for a touring musician. Given the over-saturated music performance market in Austin, this practice has become profitable to venue owners and concert organisers. Young aspiring artists already face financial barriers that preclude them from recording in a professional studio or benefitting from the services of a marketing team. Despite hip-hop's global appeal, aspiring artists continue to face racial and ethnic barriers that impede their career ambitions. Thus, pay-to-play represents another obstacle that aspiring and independent musicians must face in their journeys to creative work.

The AMX collective was created to help hip-hop artists manoeuvre around these obstacles and clear pathways for them to pursue their interests in creative work more generally and hip-hop production specifically.

Navigating the New Music Economy

The young musicians we met from the AMX collective were all striving artists. No one had a recording contract. Most of the artists we met could not afford to record music in a professional studio. And while many of them made music they laboured over in the shadows of the industry, they were forced to navigate the contradictions of the digital music economy with creativity and grit. Like many in their generation, the rappers, DJs, and producers from AMX are empowered by a do-it-yourself (DIY) approach to media production that employs clever workarounds as strategies for accessing the resources necessary to pursue their aspirations to make music. The DIY approach has been at the core of the hip-hop movement since its origins in post-industrial New York City back in the 1970s (Chang, 2005; Watkins, 2005). This movement continues to inspire young people around the world, particularly those from underrepresented and minority groups (Watkins, 2009). Many of the innovative practices that we discuss in this and the previous chapter—the hustle ethos, savvy use of technology, and cultivation of social and human capital—are enduring features of hip-hop (Watkins, 2005, 2019). Because hip-hop has been long considered outside the mainstream, hip-hop artists have been forced to invent ways to practice and sustain their creative labour.

Re-appropriating the turntable as a musical instrument, distributing music through mixtapes, building sound systems, and creating graffiti art are some of the inventive ways young people have participated in the production of hip-hop culture over the years. These youth-driven innovations have been the result of entrepreneurial activities that blur the lines between play and work or the cultural margins and mainstream centre and, thus, allow youth of colour to 'turn forms of play into paid labor' (Kelley, 1997). Since its humble origins, hip-hop has long been a source of innovation and 'aspirational labour.' Among the many participants in AMX, the aspiration has been, for example, to find opportunities for creative expression and a modicum of control over one's life and career trajectory. Although these entrepreneurial activities have not always allowed youth to make a living, they have enabled them to build alternative innovation ecosystems, grow their social networks, and exercise agency in their adoption of technology. Moreover, these innovative practices forge open pathways for youth to develop a range of technical and creative skills that produce some ancillary benefits. Those benefits include the chance to craft new pathways to what they perceive as more fulfilling work and the ability to express themselves and enrich their lives through creative endeavours.

It is precisely by building on the legacy of innovation and entrepreneurship in hip-hop that members of the AMX collective have designed their own innovation ecosystem to establish opportunities to pursue their creative ambitions as rappers, DJs, and music producers in a digital music economy marked by emergent opportunities and limitations.

Making a career as a musician is difficult. As the Austin Music Census—a data-driven assessment of Austin's commercial music economy—reveals, very few artists actually make a living as full-time musicians (Titan Music Group, 2015). A decisive majority (78 percent) of musicians either have to work outside of the music industry (56 percent), work in other roles inside of the industry (15 percent), are students (2.7 percent), or unemployed (3.5 percent). Most Austin musicians live in poverty-like conditions and receive very little support from public institutions. According to the Music Census, even the musicians who have part-time (20 percent) and full-time jobs outside the industry (50 percent) make less than $25,000 annually—a figure that falls well below the mean annual wage for living in the Austin metropolitan area.

As one aspiring rapper from AMX explained to us, making a living in Austin as an independent musician is hard. He said, 'I just think about this day and age, it's really hard to make a living just doing music alone, especially since, you know, we used to have CDs back in the day, but now everything is digital.' He explained that selling physical copies of your music is much more difficult in the new music streaming ecosystem that has rapidly become the norm for music consumption.

> If I'm selling physical CDs people are like, 'I can just go online and listen to it.' And so, I feel like most of where the money's coming from it's, like, shows, tours, you know? That's where most of the money's really coming from. If you're not doing that, the only other way you can actually make profit is by selling merchandise.

This new reality compels artists on the margins of the industry to invent new models for music making and income-earning opportunities.

The young rapper's insights point to one of the many striking contradictions that shape the new music economy. Even as digital technologies—music apps, music streaming, music-making software, and social media—have transformed the music industry, most artists recognise that the most certain ways to earn money in music are through 'old-school' enterprises, such as live performances and merchandise. In other words, physical labour remains vital even in a digital economy. The innovation ecosystem that AMX participants built was a testament to the fact that even as many of these artists recorded music in makeshift studios like their bedrooms with a laptop and music-making software and used social media channels like Facebook, Twitter, and SoundCloud to share their music and build an audience, the chances of earning income from their creative labour depended, principally, on the execution of traditional forms of labour, such as live performances, networking, and selling merchandise.

This fact explains why the AMX founders invested their limited resources in building a collective that cultivated distinct forms of physical, human, social, and technological capital to support a community of artists seeking very distinct pathways into music and creative careers.

Building an Innovation Ecosystem for Aspirational Musicians

If there was one endeavour that stood out in the innovation ecosystem the members of AMX created, it was the weekly 'open mic' night that the organisation coordinated. Every Tuesday evening from 10:00 pm to 2:00 am, aspiring rappers, DJs, beat makers, and hip-hop fans gathered in a small local event venue to participate in the open mic. The AMX co-founders believed that by adopting the open mic format, they could mobilise local hip-hop artists and support the various forms of music production that were percolating underground.

An open mic set usually involves rappers or beat makers coming out to display their rhyming or production skills in front of a live audience. The event is open because rather than schedule established artists, open mics are primarily for aspiring artists looking to hone their skills, build their reputations, or breakthrough. Each open mic event is contingent upon artists showing up and volunteering to perform.

The founders of AMX imagined a weekly event that allowed local hip-hop artists to perform, experiment, and network. For instance, each open mic night featured roughly 20 artists who performed on stage in five-minute sets. The open mic night was also a chance for rappers, DJs, and beat makers to experiment with a new performance style, rhyme, or music mix. In addition, the weekly event established a regular opportunity for artists who worked in isolation to connect with other artists and build their social networks. At first glance, the open mic night consisted primarily of the artists who performed on stage. But as we probed deeper, the dynamics of the open mic night produced outcomes that extended far beyond what was visible on the surface.

Hip-hop artists were spread across distant areas of the city. As one of the AMX co-founders, explained, 'It was tough to contact people. People were kind of all over and dispersed.' Like the indie game collective that we profiled in the previous chapter, one of the main challenges facing the founders of AMX was to create a solution that organised the isolated talent into a coherent community.

The lack of organisation not only stifled individuals but also limited the broader community's capacity to grow its collective creative potential and influence. The co-founder explained the purpose of the open mic this way: 'There needs to be a place where everyone can come, be together, and meet.' The central organising principle was the idea that a more coherent community could foster more creativity and opportunity.

The notion of a 'scene' in music, broadly defined as a localised community of artists and audiences that come together for making, circulating, and consuming music, entered the popular imagination in the 20th century. Journalists, academics, and practitioners have consistently used this term to describe the music activities and genres that take place in a particular city or town. Scholars, for instance, have studied 'scenes' in order to understand the cultural practices, behavioural dynamics, and networks of music production, reception, and distribution usually driven by youth and independent artists clustered in a specific geographic location (Straw, 1991; Bennet, 2000; Smith & Maughan, 1998; see also Chapter 4).

Although researchers have pointed out the emergence of translocal (scattered local scenes interconnected through communication and around a distinctive music genre) and virtual scenes (individuals scattered across physical spaces creating a scene through the Internet), local music scenes continue to be important for independent artists (Kruse, 2010; Peterson & Bennet, 2004). Geography and locality matter because they are powerful sources of identity, allow people to come together in close proximity to each other, and establish the conditions for creative expression and collaboration.

Informal Innovation

Innovation is also a social process of collective action developed in environments that foster creativity. According to Katz and Wagner (2014, p. 2), 'Innovation is when new or improved ideas, products, services, technologies, or processes create new market demand or cutting-edge solutions to economic, social and environmental challenges.'

As Peter Tschmuck has argued in *Creativity and Innovation in the Music Industry* (2012),

> Innovation is the process of the emergence of a novelty, as well as the alteration of existing routines. During this process, novelty materializes in various forms, such as in the form of new products and production processes but also in the form of social institutions, including new social fields of action. Accompanying the process of innovation, creativity is a collective process of action in which novelty is recognized and accepted. (. . .) Innovation happens only when the creative process has begun, and novelty was construed as different from the already known.
>
> (pp. 223–224)

In this analysis, we posit that the creation of AMX and the ecosystem it fostered is an expression of innovation insofar as it was a novel solution to a social and economic challenge. First, AMX confronted the challenge of transforming an isolated, ineffective, and largely unrecognised community of hip-hop creatives into a connected, active, and visible community that fostered opportunities to make music. Second, AMX confronted the need to build a culture that supported the development of skills—networking, live performance, music production, merchandising—that are requisites in a rapidly evolving music industry. Moreover, this articulation of innovation took shape outside of the formal infrastructures—local bookers, venues, festivals, and production studios—that drive Austin's thriving local music economy.

AMX participants had to design their own showcases, networks, and pathways to local venues to find creative and income-earning opportunities. As a result, we called their inventive tactics an expression of *informal innovation*—that is, a mode of innovation that took place completely outside the conventional corridors of power and influence in Austin's local music economy. Among other things, informal innovation requires hustle, imagination, and inventiveness.

Informal Innovation Labs

Innovation labs are typically associated with big corporations, downtown tech hubs, and universities. In our fieldwork, we began to think of the open mic event as an informal innovation lab. How was the open mic event an innovation lab? We answer this question first by explaining what innovation labs do.

Among other things, innovation labs expose individuals to diverse expertise, a key feature in the development of new ideas, products, and services. The exchange of ideas, knowledge, and information suggest that innovation is an inherently social and collaborative enterprise. Moreover, innovation labs are spaces where inventors, designers, and creators can receive feedback and support. Also, innovation labs offer a space to learn through experimentation—that is, trial and error or 'learning by doing.' Importantly, innovation labs are safe spaces to try something new, fail, and iterate. Moreover, innovation labs provide the opportunity to transform an idea into something tangible. They are, in effect, spaces to create and build the future (Watkins, 2019).

We likened the open mic night to an innovation lab and believe it illustrates how young people are transforming unconventional spaces into opportunities to pursue their creative aspirations. 'Really what this is about is about kids trying to cut their teeth on the craft they love,' noted one of the regular open mic attendees. Functioning much like an innovation lab, the open mic event presents the opportunity to learn through creative activity that is hands-on, experiential, and social.

We also noticed the savvy ways that young people learned to make media. This was an indication of how they cultivated human capital or the capacity to learn new things that encouraged their music-making aspirations. Many of the skills that are required to produce the media that circulated among AMX participants, including digital tracks, mixtapes, videos, and merchandise, were developed informally—that is, outside of any formal learning context, such as school. In the innovation labs—the open mic night, homemade studios, the Internet—that AMX artists accessed, they practiced skills such as creativity, problem solving, design, and entrepreneurship. Our fieldwork suggests that the innovation ecosystems that young people are building are notable as much for how they support learning and skill building as for actual creative labour and expression.

The Geography of Creative Work

Because most young people looking to turn a passion project or interest into a career lack economic capital, they do not have access to more formal or established physical assets, such as an office, lab, or studio. In our fieldwork, we observed how young people across various sectors turned to a variety of alternative spaces—community labs, old buildings, coworking spaces, coffee shops, event spaces, and their bedrooms—to practice innovation (Watkins, 2019). The AMX artists that we observed adopted a unique mix of venues, including event spaces, bars, parking lots, and coffee houses to gather, create, perform, and grow their social and creative capital.

In this section, we highlight one specific physical resource—an event space—that became the setting for the weekly open mic. AMX participants used this event venue for capital-enhancing activities, such as skill building, networking, information sharing, and generating income-earning opportunities. The crowds that formed during open mic night presented abundant opportunities to socialise and network with other open mic night attendees via the exchange of information, knowledge, and support for fledgling creative types and entrepreneurs. In addition to facilitating the exchange of ideas and information, the social features of the venue established a space to exchange some of the goods and services open mic attendees produced—namely, music and merchandise.

We noticed on many occasions how the open mic participants set up informal, pop-up mini stores during the event. Similar to the indie game developers we discussed in the previous chapter, members of the AMX collective practiced their own pop-up economy, using the open mic venue as a space to engage in their own gift (Hyde, 1983) and market economy. AMX members exchanged flyers, business cards, and other promotional materials. Some of the participants sold their music and merchandise (e.g. T-shirts).

In this economy, mixtapes were important. Mixtapes have a long history in hip-hop and have been used as a vehicle for creative expression, reputation building, and income (Driscoll, 2009). Mixtapes are a physical manifestation of an emcee or DJ's creative labour and career aspirations. This particular innovation usually involves recording rap lyrics over mixed beats (found or bought online or provided by a local producer), printing CDs, and designing visual and audio-visual materials to promote the final product. Usually produced independently and in homemade studios, mixtapes are often a first step towards starting a career as a hip-hop emcee or DJ.

During our fieldwork, we saw many rappers carrying their mixtape CDs in their backpacks and sharing them with the attendees at open mic night and other shows. Although they usually gave the CDs away for free, artists occasionally requested donations to support their creative pursuits. By the end of our fieldwork, we had collected more than 60 mixtapes CDs from our participant observations at the AMX open mic, illustrating how active AMX members were and how hard they laboured in pursuit of their music-making aspirations.

The pop-up economy model also manifests itself in the virtual world. Take, for example, the entrepreneurial efforts of two aspiring MCs we met. They both designed personal websites that allowed them to aggregate their content across multiple social media platforms. Both rappers used their websites to showcase their music, photographs, videos, and set up an online 'store.' One of the artists dedicated his online store to selling

T-shirts. The other set up an elaborate online store in which he sold albums and T-shirts at a fixed rate as well as mixtapes and single songs with a 'pay-what-you-want' pricing system. He also set up an 'automatic donations' feature on his website, which invited fans to support his music career by contributing five dollars every month. It was, in some respects, a modified version of the crowdfunding model that has become popular in the DIY economy. Efforts to generate income in both the physical setting of the open mic event and the virtual setting of the Internet highlights the degree to which young aspiring artists move fluidly across physical and virtual worlds in their journey towards creative work.

As several researchers have pointed out, entrepreneurial activities have become essential to the development of independent music careers in the new economy (Tschmuck, 2017; Hracs & Leslie, 2014; Wikström, 2009 Hracs, 2016; Haijen, 2016). The independent artist as an entrepreneur has become a model for creative industry careers in a neoliberal context characterised by precarious labour (Chapman, 2013; Speers, 2016). However, critics charge that big tech companies exploit the 'labour' that users devote to social media platforms for massive financial gain. This is a notable critique and one that raises questions about digital labour, ownership of user-generated content, and the economics and ethics of social media (Andrejevic, 2008; Fuchs, 2013; Scholz, 2012). It is quite likely that the owners of social media platforms benefitted more, at least financially, from all of this social media labour than the artists.

Cultivating Social Capital

Social capital assets are essential for the process of innovation because they are, among other things, vital instruments of information, trust, and opportunity. As we noted above, one of the main motivations for creating AMX was to build an organisation that enabled artists who were physically dispersed to experience greater community and connectivity. The AMX collective was composed of artists who shared an affinity for hip-hop and the challenges of kickstarting their music-making aspirations.

The weekly open mic was a 'social capital hub.' More specifically, the event was intentional in its efforts to grow an innovation ecosystem premised on the frequent exchange of informational and material resources related to finding pathways into the local music economy. For example, it was not uncommon for artists attending the open mic to access information about bookers and venues. Participants regularly shared information about particular venues in town that were amenable to booking upstart hip-hop rappers and DJs. There was a constant exchange of material resources too. During the open mic night, a photographer might agree to conduct a photo session with a rapper who was looking to create a publicity packet. Both parties benefitted from this social transaction. The rapper was able to gain promotional materials while the photographer was able to add another client to her portfolio. Like the meet-ups that we discuss in the previous chapter, the open mic nights were a regular opportunity to nourish social ties that provided access to resources that AMX artists would have struggled to find on their own.

This practice of reciprocity and the sense of belonging fostered trust, a key dimension of social capital. Trust can strengthen the opportunities for the development of both 'strong' and 'weak' ties (Granovetter, 1995). An example of a strong tie may be someone a person knows, such as a family friend. By contrast, a weak tie may be a friend of a friend. Here we focus briefly on the benefits associated with the cultivation of weak ties in the AMX open mic event.

The investment in weak ties was aided by social media. Members of the AMX collective used Facebook, Twitter, and SoundCloud to develop ties that reached beyond local geographic boundaries and the strong ties available to them. AMX members leveraged social platforms to widen their access to information and expertise related to their music-making aspirations. As we discuss in greater detail in our discussion of the technological assets used in the AMX collective, members' active presence in the virtual spaces of online platforms further accentuates the vitality of weak ties, a critical resource in social relations.

The weak ties cultivated by AMX members were a vivid reminder of the frequently stated adage that when trying to get ahead in life, 'it's not necessarily what you know, but who you know.' By providing a space and an event to gather regularly with other hip-hop artists and engage in conversation and mutual exchange, the meet-up was an important opportunity for young artists to expand who they knew in both the informal and formal spheres of the local music economy.

Hip-hop innovation has always been social. Crews, cliques, and 'homies' (i.e. friends and neighbours) have long been at the root of hip-hop's entrepreneurial identity and legacy. These social ties have been pursued by groups of passionate youth that come together in order to build vibrant spaces where they can learn, socialise, ideate, and engage in the practices of experimentation and collaboration in various forms of cultural production, including music, art, film, and fashion. Those spaces have become fertile terrain for building social connections and finding support. As one of the co-founders of AMX explained during an interview, 'The history of hip-hop is written by people hanging out together, talking about what they are into, and deciding to do stuff together.'

Creating With Tech

In the previous chapter, we explained how technological advances have lowered the barrier to entry in the production of high-quality games, inspiring a vibrant DIY movement in the production of interactive media. Technological advances have long been a key feature in the production of indie music, making it possible for artists not attached to major corporate labels to practice innovation in the production and distribution of music. Members of the AMX collective were quite savvy when it came to using the mix of technologies that were available to them, including laptop computers, audio software, and social media.

The laptop computer was a widely adopted technological asset in the AMX collective. Laptops serve as de facto studios for many aspirational musicians. Most musicians just starting on their journey into creative work cannot afford the fees required to rent out access to studio space and the music producers who run them. Many of the AMX artists that we interviewed used laptop computers to create, store, and share music. The lightweight design of laptops makes them an ideal tool for music artists who seldom have a dedicated space to make music. The ability to access previously recorded beats, craft songs, and test new recordings via the laptop provided both a labour efficient and cost-effective mechanism for producing content.

Some AMX artists built basic production studios in their homes with the laptop serving as the anchor. These homemade studios typically included a microphone, speakers, headphones, and, in some instances, an external soundcard and midi keyboards. Several artists have purchased some of the affordable audio production software that allows them to record and produce songs, create mixtapes, and record DJ beats and mixes.

Access to affordable and free audio software like GarageBand and Audacity supplied tools to produce studio quality beats and songs from a homemade studio. Like many other young media producers, AMX members took full advantage of the availability of free multimedia software and the large repository of audio, images, and videos flowing across the Internet. As a result, they extended their remix practices to other kinds of media. Besides making music with their computers, AMX artists also used the suite of tech available to them to design promotional flyers, compose photos, and edit music videos. The content that was generated with their laptops was used to promote their work and their skills.

Not surprisingly, social media channels were one of the most important technological assets in the AMX innovation ecosystem. Social media was widely used among the aspiring artists that participated in the music collective. Through their adoption of social media AMX members engaged in a mix of creative and social practices.

Virtually every rapper, MC, and producer that we met during our fieldwork maintained an online presence. Some of the more popular channels included Facebook, Twitter, Tumblr, and Instagram. AMX members used social media to practice the presentation of the 'creative self.' Drawing from Irving Goffman's (1959) idea of the 'presentation of self in everyday life,' researchers have applied his framework to an analysis of social media behaviours (boyd & Ellison, 2007). Here we suggest that AMX and other aspirational labourers present a 'creative self' in their journey towards creative careers. This particular mode of identity work is designed to assert some degree of control over how an artist is perceived by peers, fans, and potential partners. Managing the presentation of the creative self includes developing personal websites, digital portfolios, and social media personas, which make the aspirational identities of artists and entrepreneurs more material.

Managing the creative self via social media poses some notable challenges. It was common for AMX members to use multiple social channels, which meant navigating multiple online communities. Even though social media is often treated as a monolith in the popular press and public discourse, each channel develops its own community norms, style of communication, and repertoires of participation. Thus, in order to derive even a minor degree of value via social media, an artist who was active on Facebook, Twitter, and SoundCloud had to become knowledgeable about the norms and communities that shape those respective channels. This required devoting time and energy to learning the distinct nuances and rules of engagement via the different social media in order to cultivate a presence and a community around their creative labour.

Social media was also used to socialise and collaborate with other artists. One AMX member told us that social media has helped him to not only share his music beyond the local market he has ties to but also to connect to a broader network of artists. He explained it this way. 'Technology has helped me to get my music out, definitely, like, using the Internet, Sound Cloud, Reverb Nation, Facebook, Band Camp, and all the different outlets for artists to put their music on.' This same AMX participant added, 'social media makes it easier just to spread your music [to] people in different regions. And so social media has definitely been, like, a plus now that everything's digital in this age for music.'

For many aspiring artists, social media is an opportunity to cultivate ties to artists and information flows that may be inaccessible otherwise. During our fieldwork, we learned that young artists use social media to expand their access to a greater diversity of creative types and sources of expertise. Studies of social networks suggest that it is not necessarily the size of a social network that generates benefits, but rather the diversity of a network. In other words, knowing a greater diversity of people is generally more beneficial than simply knowing a lot of people. Sociologists call this *network extensity* (Lin, 2001). Take, for example, the adoption of SoundCloud by AMX participants, the audio sharing platform created in 2010.

Young aspiring and independent musicians were among the first class of creative types to understand the value of SoundCloud (Watkins, 2019). They used the platform to form communities that shared interests in independent music and artistry. In the AMX community, SoundCloud was used to connect to other hip-hop artists, solicit feedback on their songs, and offer feedback to other artists. SoundCloud was more than a place for AMX artists to build up their portfolio of music; it was also a place to build important social ties. These connections provided feedback on their music, information about the underground and independent music circuits, and companionship. As one AMX member noted in a reference to SoundCloud, 'It has helped me expand the social base in my music network just by me being able to talk to other artists and other artists reaching out to me for songs.'

Conclusion: Creative Labour and the Pursuit of Opportunity and Dignity

This chapter suggests that young people's journeys into creative work are complex. On the one hand, the decision to pursue a creative career with limited resources was an expression of resilience. On the other, the chance to turn a DIY enterprise into a full-time gig is elusive at best. Most of the artists we met did not make a living pursuing their creative passions and aspirations. For many, their creative labour was a side hustle, defined elsewhere by Watkins (2019, p. 11) 'as an improvisational and creative assertion of agency in the face of uncertain circumstances.' Most of the AMX artists held down jobs, when they were fortunate enough to be employed. Thus, music was something that they did in the off hours, late at night, weekends, or whenever they could find the time, energy, and resources required to pursue a career in music. One participant in the AMX collective described his music-making efforts this way.

> My balance between my music life and the life outside of music is a struggle. It's definitely a struggle because, in the daytime, I have a job where I work. And then, after I get off of work, I do music at night. . . . So I live kind of a triple life almost. And it's just really hard.

Many of the AMX artists understood that they would never reach the celebrity achieved by Drake or Jay-Z. As a result, they articulated more modest aspirations. Many artists told us that they would be satisfied with earning enough income to simply continue making and performing music. Their goals included meeting and collaborating with other artists, building a small but loyal community around their music, and performing in local and regional music venues. AMX artists certainly wanted to make money from their music-making ventures. The hip-hop collective was an inventive resource to support their career aspirations. But more than anything, the AMX collective functioned like a training ground for young artists to grow their social and human capital. Whereas social capital allowed them to connect to other hip-hop creatives, the development of human capital afforded them opportunities to improve their performance and music production skills.

As we will see in the next chapter, creative work was an opportunity to become a part of a community and make something—a song or piece of merchandise—which generated enormous personal fulfilment and optimism in the face of employment circumstances that seldom offered opportunities for creativity and mobility. One AMX participant explained it this way: 'What I want to accomplish with my music is to express myself and my craft. . . . It's not the money. I really do it for the love and the passion for my craft.'

The overwhelming majority of the young people that we met held aspirations of a career in music. A lot of the practices we observed resembled what some refer to as 'aspirational labour' (Duffy, 2017) or 'hope labour' (Kuehn & Corrigan, 2013). Although technology lowers the barrier to entry in the music industry, the barriers to success have not been lowered. In fact, in a culture where everyone is a media producer making a living in music, for example, may be even more challenging in the hyperconnected and media-saturated world that we live in.

As Watkins (2019) notes, many young people pursue passion projects and side hustles mainly as a means of securing access to more rewarding creative and civic selves. In other words, the journey into creative work has grown more complex and does not necessarily represent an effort to achieve wealth and celebrity. Instead, our fieldwork suggests that many young people view the pursuit of creative work as a way to find opportunity and dignity in a society and economy where both are in short supply.

References

Anderson, C. (2006). *The long tail: Why the future of business is selling less of more*. New York, NY: Hyperion.

Andrejevic, M. (2008). Mining the wealth of online communities. *Soundings, 39*, 75–86. Retrieved from www.lwbooks.co.uk/soundings

Baym, N. (2010). Rethinking the music industry. *Popular Communication*, Special issue on the recession, 8(3), 177–180.

Bennett, A. (2000). *Popular music and youth culture: Music, identity and place*. London: Macmillan Press.

boyd, d., & Ellison, N. (2007). Social network sites: Definition, history, and scholarship. *Computer-Mediated Communication, 13*(1), 210–230.

Chang, J. (2005). *Can't stop won't stop: A history of the hip-hop generation*. New York, NY: St. Martin's Press.

Chapman, D. (2013). The "one-man band" and entrepreneurial selfhood in neoliberal culture. *Popular Music, 32*(3), 451–470.

De Peuter, G. (2011). Creative economy and labor precarity: A contested convergence. *Journal of Communication Inquiry, 35*(4), 417–425.

Driscoll, K. (2009). *Stepping your game up: Technical innovation among young people of color in hip-hop*. MIT Masters thesis in Comparative Media Studies.

Duffy, B. E. (2017). *(Not) getting paid to do what you love: Gender, social media, and aspirational work*. New Haven, CT: Yale University Press.

Frenette, A. (2013). Making the intern economy: Role and career challenges of the music industry intern. *Work and Occupations, 40*(4), 364–397.

Frenette, A. (2016). "Working at the candy factory": The limits of nonmonetary rewards in record industry careers. In B. J. Hracs, M. Seman, & T. Virani (Eds.), *The production and consumption of music in the digital age* (pp. 85–99). New York, NY: Routledge.

Fuchs, C. (2013). Class and exploitation on the Internet. In T. Scholz (Ed.), *Digital labor: The Internet as playground and factory* (pp. 149–164). New York, NY and London, UK: Routledge.

Gill, R., & Pratt, A. C. (2008). In the social factory? Immaterial labour, precariousness and cultural work. *Theory, Culture & Society, 25*(7–8), 1–30.

Goffman, I. (1959). *The presentation of self in everyday life.* New York, NY: Anchor.

Granovetter, M. (1995). *Getting a job: A study of contacts and careers* (2nd ed.). Chicago, IL: University of Chicago Press.

Haijen, J. R. (2016). Hip-Hop tunity: The production and consumption of music in the digital age. In B. J. Hracs, M. Seman, & T. Virani (Eds.), *The production and consumption of music in the digital age* (pp. 71–84). New York, NY: Routledge.

Hracs, B. J. (2016). Working harder and working smarter: The survival strategies of contemporary independent musicians. In B. J. Hracs, M. Seman, & T. Virani (Eds.), *The production and consumption of music in the digital age* (pp. 42–55). New York, NY: Routledge.

Hracs, B. J., & Leslie, D. (2014). Aesthetic labour in creative industries: The case of independent musicians in Toronto. *Area, 46,* 66–73.

Hyde, L. (1983). *The gift: Imagination and the erotic life of property.* New York, NY: Vintage.

Katz, B., & Wagner, J. (2014). *The rise of innovation districts: A new geography of innovation in America.* Metropolitan Policy Program at Brookings. Washington, DC: Brookings Institution.

Kelley, R. D. G. (1997). Looking to get paid: How some black put culture to work. In *Yo' mama's disfunktional!: Fighting the culture wars in urban America.* Boston, MA: Beacon Press.

Kruse, H. (2010). Local identity and independent music scenes, online and off. *Popular Music and Society, 33*(5), 625–639.

Kuehn, K., & Corrigan, T. F. (2013). Hope labor: The role of employment prospects in online social production. *Political Economy of Communication, 1*(1), 9–25.

Leyshon, A. (2014). *Reformatted: Code, networks, and the transformation of the music industry.* Oxford, UK and New York, NY: Oxford University Press.

Lin, N. (2001). *Social capital: A theory of social structure and action.* Cambridge, UK: Cambridge University Press.

Neilson, B., & Rossiter, N. (2005). From precarity to precariousness and back again: Labour, life and unstable networks. *The Fibreculture Journal, 5.* Retrieved from http://five.fibreculturejournal.org/fcj-022-from-precarity-to-precariousness-and-back-again-labour-life-and-unstable-networks/

Peterson, R. A., & Bennett, A. (2004). Introducing music scenes. In R. A. Peterson & A. Bennett (Eds.), *Music scenes: Local, translocal, and virtual* (pp. 1–16). Nashville, TN: Venderbilt University Press.

Pratt, A. C. (2000). New media, the new economy and new spaces. *Geoforum, 31*(4), 425–436.

Scholz, T. (Ed.). (2012). *Digital labor: The Internet as playground and factory.* New York, NY: Routledge.

Sehgal, K. (2018, January 26). Spotify and Apple Music should become record labels so musicians can make a fair living. *CNBC.* Retrieved from www.cnbc.com/2018/01/26/how-spotify-apple-music-can-pay-musicians-more-commentary.html

Smith, R. J., & Maughan, T. (1998). Youth culture and the making of the post-Fordist economy: Dance music in contemporary Britain. *Journal of Youth Studies, 1*(2), 211–228.

Speers, L. (2016). From artist to entrepreneur: The working lives of London-based rappers. In B. J. Hracs, M. Seman, & T. Virani (Eds.), *The production and consumption of music in the digital age* (pp. 71–84). New York, NY: Routledge.

Straw, W. (1991). Systems of articulation, logics of change: Communities and scenes in popular music. *Cultural Studies, 5*(3), 368–388.

Titan Music Group. (2015). *The city of Austin economic development department's music & entertainment division.* Austin, TX: Titan Music Group. Retrieved from www.titanmusicgroup.com

Towse, R. (2010). Creativity, copyright and the creative industries paradigm. *KYKLOS, 63*(3), 461–478.

Tschmuck, P. (2012). *Creativity and innovation in the music industry.* Berlin, Germany: Springer.

Tschmuck, P. (2017). *The economics of music.* Newcastle upon Tyne, UK: Agenda Publishing.

Watkins, S. C. (2005). *Hip hop matters: Pop culture, politics, and the struggle for the soul of a movement.* Boston, MA: Beacon Press.

Watkins, S. C. (2009, October 12). Why hip-hop is like no other. *Foreign Policy.* Retrieved from https://foreignpolicy.com/2009/10/12/why-hip-hop-is-like-no-other/

Watkins, S. C. (2019). *Don't knock the hustle: Young creatives, tech ingenuity, and the making of a new innovation economy.* Boston, MA: Beacon Press.

Wikström, P. (2013). *The music industry: Music in the cloud.* Cambridge, UK: Polity.

4 Learning Creative Identities in Filmmaking

The Dubious Pleasures of Precarity

Julian Sefton-Green

> More qualitative longitudinal research is needed into the evolution of creative aspirations and how they are affected by both the structures of feeling in an age of precarity and the specifics of individual adaptations to, and within, particular creative industries.
>
> (Morgan, Wood, & Nelligan, 2013, p. 412)

This chapter draws on a series of interviews with young people mainly in their 20s and mainly from ethnic minorities, all of whom had worked, were working as, or aspired to work as filmmakers in London, UK in 2015/2016. Following Morgan et al.'s (2013) aforementioned suggestion, this research tells stories of perseverance, exclusion, commitment, achievement, insecurity, and uncertainty. As these life histories—or creative biographies (Gill, 2009)—unfolded during their telling, they revealed both personal or individual and structural dimensions. The personal stories locate the tellers within their neighbourhoods or communities and recount making do at particular moments—filming rap contests over a summer, the serendipity of an interpersonal contact that led to a job opportunity, and so on; inevitably, they recount random chance, contingency, good or bad luck. At a structural level, these individuals reflected on how being black in Britain, and not middle class, hindered possibilities for employment at the same time as they facilitated niche work opportunities. The life histories give insight into the struggles involved in developing expertise, settling on a career, developing a professional profile, and working in an ever-changing marketplace for film and other moving image media.

Whereas the conventional pipeline taking young people from education or training into work acknowledges the stresses of transition (just as they are presumed to operate during the move from dependency on the family into adulthood [Furlong & Cartmel, 2006]), these creative biographies, in effect, describe an almost continuous transition process— a seemingly endless stage of uncertainty with associated stress. Rather than the idea of passing through a gateway into work, of building a life around a framework that has key entry moments of competitive intensity, these young people have reconfigured that framework to one of an ongoing hustle. The creative biographies recount a repetitive process of project-based experiences, reliance on peer-based solidarity whilst trying to secure the next chance, and balancing an unequal and uneven flow of income with grand ambitions. Whilst the term 'hustle' might adequately describe dimensions of performance, persuasion, and entrepreneurial drive, it doesn't quite account for an existential element where individuals' sense of values, purpose, and meaning is bound up in the identity they created for themselves as young filmmakers.

The idea of continuous transition clearly has structural resonance with the more widespread analytic concept of precarity (Standing, 2016). However, as noted in the book's introduction, we would be cautious as to how far this concept helps us to understand the work lives this group of young people were building for themselves. This limitation has both to do with the field of activity—filmmaking as part of the creative and cultural industries—and these young people's socially marginal position within the wider society. As the introduction to this volume outlined, there is considerable literature exploring the relationship between precarity and creative labour that investigates how forms of employment in the creative and cultural industries are providing a blueprint for changing modes of work (Guile, 2006) and how they operate within severe labour markets (Ashton, 2013, 2014, 2015; Banks & Oakley, 2015; Oakley & O'Brien, 2016). The way that film projects are funded, underpinning the structural economics of this field relies on a surplus of qualified labour (Caves, 2000), so it is a mistake to imagine that young entrants could depend on any form of regular career progression—as if there might be a norm in line with conventional principles of transition. What is interesting here is how the creative biographies show the young person learning how to behave and act in this demanding set of economic circumstances without them necessarily imagining that this is only a preparatory stage in a longer normative trajectory. At the same time, the fact that these young people came from ethnic minority and often low-income households meant that they were always aware of the challenges facing participation in a high-stakes, high-reward industry—that chances for people like themselves were always likely to be few and far between. Whilst on the surface, it might be tempting to see these biographies simply as examples of managing new kinds of precarious labour markets (Peters & Bulut, 2011) in straitened economic circumstances (Allen, 2015), we want to make the case that they also exemplify an attitude towards the aspiration of a career as perpetual career building where the resource of the person her or himself is both the object and subject of capital investment. Furthermore, the narrative work undertaken through the process of data collection—as these young people constructed the creative biography for us and themselves—showed a commitment to an artistic or creative practice whose value to the individual seemed to outweigh its practical plausibility.

Work as Participation

Although the nature of work is currently undergoing a theoretical reconceptualisation (Srnicek & Williams, 2016) primarily because of changes in knowledge sharing, automation and globalisation (Baldwin, 2016), classically, work is understood as the exchange of labour in a marketplace. However, filmmaking meant more to these young people than simply a way of earning a living, and therefore, embracing it as a vocation, or way of life, required them to constantly calibrate any sense of themselves they might have as possessing an identity within the filmmaking field (see Bourdieu, 1990, 1993). We want to show that this concern with identity was as much their 'work' as the work they might do as filmmakers. For this reason, the chapter is structured around participation in three kinds of 'fields of practice' in the Bourdieuian sense. The first of these can best be described as a 'scene.' Following early work by Will Straw (Straw, 1991) and then a later investigation (Woo, Rennie, & Poyntz, 2014), the idea of a scene, albeit a loose theoretical formulation, captures a cultural grouping or activity or performance or coming together characterised by a collective sense of purpose and engagement as understood by its participants. Participating in scenes is often a kind of 'free labour,' and although the cultural scenes Straw described predate the participatory culture of the Internet, the same concerns about self-exploitation pertain. The concept of 'free' or 'immaterial' labour (Terranova, 2004) online and in scenes is useful for our young filmmakers because, as we will see, they often describe their participation in filmmaking as a kind of gift exchange—where their work is unpaid in monetary terms, or at least underpaid—but the rewards in terms of participating in the scene and belonging to its community clearly count. Indeed, making films is, from this perspective, a way of participating in a local scene economy. This is frequently distinct from the ways that participating in a scene—making videos of the local rap artist, for example—may or may not capitalise the filmmaker's future hypothetical career trajectory.

Secondly, we will find out about these young people's paid work in the film industry—that is, in more conventional types of employment. However, what emerged very quickly from these narratives is that the market for film is varied and insecure, from public relations companies that wanted 'spontaneous' footage of events for use on Facebook, to making music videos sometimes financed by drug money, to working in a junior capacity on large Hollywood or British film industry financed films. Unlike the trajectories described in the stratified film-related careers by John Thornton Caldwell (Caldwell, 2008), where individuals have a clear sense of their roles within a Hollywood company that has its place in a knowable economy, these young people had to puzzle out how one job may or may not lead to another and how to create a notion of career progression through a range of different market opportunities—themselves often insecure and contingent on precarious funding. They had to figure out the reputational benefit of building up a portfolio and of engaging in activities—often through scenes—that they felt were meaningful as opposed to the putative benefits of taking menial roles in large, more formal organisations. In this context, we can see them coming to terms with what it might mean to be a filmmaker in both formal and informal media economies (Lobato, Thomas, & Hunter, 2011), even where there were few mechanisms for labour to cross between these domains, thus creating difficulties in moving between these dimensions of the contemporary marketplace. We were also struck by how, rather than simply taking on an employee relationship with an employer as in 'having a job,' paid employment came across much more in terms of a mode of participation—of learning ways of being or behaving, as well as creating and identifying with particular aesthetic outputs.[1]

The final kind of work we observed in these young people was the effort and process that went into the activity of career building as part of their presence in the filmmaking field. Since employment as a filmmaker is reliant on a portfolio of previous work, and since new projects often have to be secured in terms of financing, having a job in the sector isn't quite like waiting for the opportunity to arise and making an application. In between paid employment, and indeed even at work on projects, our filmmakers are constantly engaged in a process of developing their careers, building up a network of contacts, and extending all kinds of social and cultural capital as a form of investment and/or reputational value. Careership (Hodkinson & Sparkes, 1997; Hodkinson, 2008) becomes its own object of endeavour; not only did our young people have to learn the mechanics of career building but also they had to tend to its growth and the social rituals and activities in which filmmaking is embedded as much as they had to demonstrate expertise in their chosen medium.

The chapter argues that rather than seeing employment in this field in simply transactional terms, as the exchange of labour in a market, it makes more sense to see these creative biographies as a form of participation in filmmaking as a social field (Bourdieu, 1990). Having a job was understood by these young people in terms of a form of social participation which in turn generated further employment. Participation was significantly a question of identity work, of operating as a character in the social field, rather than simply a question of abstractly developing expertise (with technology or aesthetics) that could be bought or sold, and this approach to skills is in contradistinction to conventional progression through academic credentials. The three fields of activity—scenes, paid employment, and career building—were for our interviewees intimately interconnected and self-reinforcing, yet we will also see that there was no rational progression between the three fields and no normative modes of development and growth to act as measures of progress.

The Creative Biographies

The data for this chapter comprised nine in-depth open-ended interviews with interviewees mainly recruited through an informal learning centre in London (Sefton-Green, 2017), with some interviewees being found through a snowballing effect. Half of the interviewees were known through other projects. The interviews themselves involved ongoing discussion of their work and life in addition to the sharing of online material such as their own websites and films. Half of the interviewees had a higher education degree but nearly all of them were the first in their families to go to university, and they were from relatively impoverished and socially marginalised social backgrounds. Discussion involved reflecting on early education experiences, entry into filmmaking, and statements of ambition and comparison with peers, as well as a detailed account of all the 'work' undertaken in film and filmmaking to date. Explicit attention was paid to the role of ethnicity, class and racism as, in a British context (as in the US), the media, and especially film and TV, are frequently critiqued for being too white and socially exclusive (O'Brien, Laurison, Miles, & Friedman, 2016; (www.nesta.org.uk/blog/interactive-map-geography-creativity-uk#comments).

Because of their participation in various scenes, most of the young people possessed a diverse rather than a specialised set of creative skills. Although one or two were solely camera operators (director of photography [DOP]), many demonstrated a digital fluency across traditionally discrete skill sets and edited, filmed and directed and were also involved in production and writing. Unlike in many studies of creative practitioners (Mayer, Banks, & Caldwell, 2009; Peiperl, Arthur, & Anand, 2002), these young people were at vulnerable stages of their careers. They hadn't experienced steady employment; their entry into the field had been through informal media, non-formal learning centres, and forms of community participation much like apprenticeship routes into journalism in the early years of the 20th century and even into television post-war. It may well be that in ten years' time, none of them will be working in this field but, we wanted to capture the workforce that is often only represented as casualties in an attritional labour market. The employment in informal media economies drew on social resources (the local postcode rap contests between neighbouring housing estates—projects in the US) and rapidly shifting technologically driven industrial practices from the (at that time) small digital cameras to the emergence of new distribution platforms such as Myspace or Facebook. This cohort worked the cutting edge of many of these commercial, technological, and social changes, and were both able to take advantage of opportunities as much as they represented a disposable and precarious workforce.[2]

Making Scenes Happen

The landmark study by Mimi Ito and her colleagues (Ito et al., 2010) into the spread, nature, and scope of young people's engagement in forms of digital culture proposed a kind of progression from 'hanging out' through more sustained 'messing around,' culminating in what she called 'geeking out.' Whilst that study did draw on some young people in their 20s, it stopped short of investigating a movement from intense, sustained interest-driven engagement into economic activity. However, these young filmmakers' participation in a range of different scenes might support Ito et al.'s argument just as they challenge normative models of progression in this field.

Interviewee Jermaine's experiences are a case in point and exemplify how scenes contain structural limits in terms of their employability. As a young man, Jermaine had fallen out of the education system for

> just hanging around with the wrong kind of people and, they were getting into like post code dramas [conflicts between neighboring estates (projects)] kind of thing, so one day I was on my way home . . . and I got stopped and I had a knife on me and that's actually what I got in trouble for.

Ending up at WAC Arts—an informal learning centre—he flourished in terms of his personal confidence and production expertise but, nevertheless, achieved no credentials nor indeed used the course as a way of getting onto a creative employment trajectory. In some ways, Jermaine seemed uninterested in turning his training into formal outcomes and saw his learning much more as a means to extend his interests in music making and to enable his participation in cultural events with his peers. So although he did courses in music technology and video which might have led to academic outcomes, he was much more engaged in utilising his newfound capabilities:

> I always produced and engineered, that was my approach. That's kind of why I wanted to go. Some of my friends started rapping and deejaying at the time and I thought to gel it altogether, if I learn how to record, you know, the talent that's around then that I can.

This was all taking place in around 2007/2008 when YouTube had not yet achieved dominance, so not only did the making music seem exciting and original, but it was also taking place in a context where business opportunities for distribution seemed up for grabs:

JERMAINE: I co-ran a YouTube-based media channel but our media was based on working with artists that were up and coming that didn't have finances behind them, so we were basically getting their content, if they had tracks, or we would record them in my studio and then we would do music videos for them so that put them out there to their online . . . kind of thing. We started our channel the same time as SBTV did . . . a similar, similar channel, the same kind of idea, but the only difference is their business model got interest from the BBC and they got a really nice deal and, you know, things elevated, elevated.

INT: So, were you just bringing together local people?

JERMAINE: Well, local talent, yes. Local talent.

Despite the possibility of commercialising these opportunities, and despite building the home studio and having access to, at that time, quite scarce technologies which were at the forefront of the ability to produce, edit and distribute high-quality output, Jermaine seemed content to participate in the scene:

> Well, I definitely wanted to elevate the people I was around and definitely be credited for that. I wouldn't say finance was my main drive because, at that time, we didn't, we couldn't really see it, of like how are we going to the money, but it was an outlet for the passion and for the message that we were all kind of trying to promote at the time. I guess [this was] . . . kind of, like a young adult's perspective on the environment and circumstance.

Although, he followed up on further education options, Jermaine never got to the stage of considering using credentials as a way of developing a career despite having quite a considerable amount of expertise and production experience. This wasn't because he couldn't imagine what work might be—WAC had introduced him to a range of entry routes and job roles:

> I was really enjoying running the studio [at WAC], and I was learning but then, we did some off-site stuff where [we went] to other studios and there was one studio we went and worked at [name-deleted]—I think he's quite famous for doing music for *The Matrix* and what not. I did a project with him, and that was really nice, and it was the Asian Dub Foundation album they were working on. I learnt loads, and then . . . about a month after that we did a project in Abbey Road, and it was a real contrast in the sense of the, technically, that should

be like for a young engineer, that's the bees knees of where you'd want to be as an engineer, but what I noticed . . . we were treated a certain way, which was really nice and welcoming, but the engineers that actually worked there, that were in-house, they didn't really seem happy and the wage they were on in comparison to the people they were working with, seemed really like, mis-matched. So it kind of gave me a different understanding of being an in-house engineer, as opposed to working for yourself as an engineer or freelancing.

In fact, Jermaine wanted a full-time role in his scene, so 'I got active with my friend, and we put together our heads and equipment and built the online media thing . . . UK Overstood.' He could envisage these experiences as a form of capital to leverage more long-term career and/or business opportunities, and was in a genuinely entrepreneurial moment as the scene itself demonstrated potential in terms of innovation in distribution mechanisms:

Because in some ways, we were kind of the first to do what we were doing, it definitely gave a big demographic of people around us, a platform and it literally, like, we did a few videos that got like ten thousand hits over a period of a week and then they went up into millions and stuff like that, and it became bigger than us to the point where we like, people were bringing us work through word of mouth. The content we were putting out, was quite a lot better than a lot of people—and they were spending a lot more money—so we kind of, in a way, we changed the game for a little while. We definitely made a mark on what was going on at that time on a visual level.

However, this assessment was framed in terms of technological efficiency rather than intellectual property or aesthetic markets:

We were using the Canon with three different lenses that allowed us to shoot at night without external lighting, so you didn't need a big rig or set up and you could just literally go with your camera, put the music on someone's phone and shoot wherever you are so that you can go on the train, a bus, Camden Town . . . [we] used to shoot those in Camden Town by the rivers down in the City. You could literally go and film two or three music videos with one or three or four artists over a period of a day. Go home and sit down and edit, and by the end of the night, because we would sometimes stay up all night editing, have two, three videos going up on line, so we got to the point where we were putting up a video every day for almost eight, nine months straight.

Between me and him in our first year and a half, we put over five hundred videos on our channel. No one had kind of done that, and especially using the equipment that we were using, with the artists that we were using that weren't very accessible to, you know, the people that really wanted to see them.

However, despite these market advantages, it was clear that Jermaine did not take advantage of the situation. He did describe a falling out with a business partner, and he did describe the difficulty of ensuring that capital that came his way came from legitimate sources, given the relationship of the music culture he was describing was, if not 'gang-based' neighbourhoods, then certainly communities resourced by the illegal sale of drugs. Yet we would also be cautious in terms of seeing his failure to take advantage of this moment in terms of either personal weakness or unpreparedness as if the only value in this experience might be how it could be framed as a stepping stone to further advantage. When he describes the whole process of monetising the cultural experience, it was clear that he understood how he might have been able to derive income from making these videos, such as when he analyses the value of the market traffic he had generated, drawing in viewers from Canada and even some Latino markets. This suggests that he was aware of what he might need to do commercially but what really came across more strongly was a sense of ethical imperatives. This was clear both in terms of the practices outlined—lending cameras, the hours spent editing, ferrying people around, uploading videos, and so on—and in terms of the reception of his videos; he portrayed this world as a gift economy in the classic Malinowskian sense:

> A lot of the artists would kind of, in some ways, we would end up calling in a favour for them so they might have been getting a video kind of on a favour basis, but then if you've introduced me to three other artists, then that would potentially pay for a video down the line. We were all kind of helping each other. . . . It kind of does make sense, because I like to see progression. I like to be part of progression. I think even when you understood, I definitely like to see myself as someone who facilitates people's progression as well as me learning and progressing through that as well.

For Jermaine, status was earned through his participation in this unusual economic moment—prior to the explosion of YouTube—and although he could see how some people benefitted more than him financially, there was little sense that he regretted that he hadn't managed to stay in this world.

When we met up with Jermaine, he told us that he was working for 'Denny's Uniforms which supplies suiting to hotel chains and restaurant chains,' a far cry from 'a creative field,' and that he was now on 'autopilot.' The world of filmmaking was very much one of personal contacts and of being part of a neighbourhood at a particular time. He could see connections with this scene to the larger marketplace of YouTube and even more role-defined careers in these creative businesses, all of which had their pleasures (and whose career pathways had been laid open for him). Yet in some sense, participating in his scene and managing to earn a living during that time through a bit of cash and keeping all that activity ongoing had been the point of it all. Critics may suggest that this existential value is a post hoc rationalisation for the barriers he had faced and a failure to progress, but this severely underestimates how playing his part in a cultural economy created purpose, value, and reward.

Trying to Parlay a Proper Job

Scenes are not only subcultural communities; they can also describe more closed or excluded markets. For example, Nathan had found work producing film for publicly funded arts organisations that wanted a mixture of visual documentation and public relations. The audience for these films is fairly stable and defined, and the funding relatively secure in that revenue to produce such work was inbuilt into these organisations' yearly budgets. Participation in this kind of scene was not a question of community membership, as was the case with Jermaine, but more like applying for a job, even though the films Nathan made, and the way they created and brought together people as audiences, were reminiscent of how a scene works.

In Nathan's case, he had to learn how to undertake complete contracts rather than simply apply for a specific role within a larger organisation, as is the case with most forms of employment. Typically—and this is clearly a structural change in labour practices as a consequence of digital technologies—he had to shoot, edit, and complete the audio, covering what would have been three or four discrete functions in the past. Nathan moved between employment with arts organisations and a relatively new genre of marketing and strategy consultancies who needed dynamic and edgy short videos for web distribution on corporate sites but also across social media. He had emerged from college very focused on 'a mix of documentation and fictional narrative style' along with a huge amount of ad hoc music-making experience and was trying to find a way of making this interest marketable. Repeatedly in interviews, he referenced his 'raw' filmmaking style quite in opposition to Toma, who we will meet next, who emphasised his competence across genres. Whilst the exact details of Nathan's rawness somehow always remained unspecified, despite his realisation that he needed to 'practice on different styles,' the relationship between the market value of his stylistic expertise and his employability is instructive.

Culturally attuned to street styles, Nathan's capacity to produce 'raw' or edgy work with a particular emphasis on jump-cut editing and access to absolutely up-to-date dubstep audio, meant that he was attractive in certain markets. Because work tended to mean the completion of projects, which was something he found gratifying and personally important rather than the simple exchange of labour in one part of the production process, Nathan had to learn how to tender for projects in this marketplace rather than simply apply for a job. Nearly two years into this way of life, he was finding it difficult both to move from a subsistence level of income and to translate this expertise into more discrete skills that would allow him to apply for employment in other editing houses or doing camera work on more advanced productions. The circumstances of digital production have given young men and women like him considerable artistic autonomy and clearly has value in a marketplace, but this actually led to a kind of ceiling in terms of how far he could parlay that expertise into more complex productions. How far 'total digital expertise' might actually hinder discrete skill/job-role expertise in the conventional labour marketplace was a challenge he was beginning to encounter when he described being rejected when applying for specific technical jobs.

More conventional job/skill roles tend to be hierarchically structured, especially in large productions (Caldwell, 2008), so the kind of project-autonomy experienced by Nathan had to be calculated against a more conventional stepping-stones approach to jobs.

Like Jermaine, Idris had been heavily involved in a local scene and, like Jermaine's experience of working in a professional recording studio, Idris too had a few days' work experience on the set of the film *Breaking and Entering* through a scheme run by industry-funded informal learning organisations to encourage diversity (see also Chapter 5). Making films as part of a 'collective' to promote his local grime (a London variant of hip-hop) scene, Idris had built up considerable expertise, like Nathan, in terms of writing, filming, and editing, and thus the work experience gave him some sense that traditional accreditation routes he lacked access to might be what he needed:

> I thought maybe I should do a course at the National Film and Television School, maybe I should do this. My options, I had so many, but in terms of actually getting in there, like National Film and Television School, it's expensive. And I couldn't get a student loan at the time, and just everything.

For a number of years, Idris ended up trapped between his inability to compete for 'jobs' because of his lack of formal credentials, his desire and ambition to participate in making films, his excessive (in labour market employability terms) expertise across a range of digital media, and his maturity in terms of participating in quite successful productions and managing the social relations involved in that. For a period of time, he tried his luck in Hollywood through a friend of his who had some success as a musician, but, however capable he was at fulfilling a range of roles in filmmaking productions, he could never quite manage to start structured employment. This was partly to do with his exclusion from conventional labour markets on account of his lack of qualifications: as when we met up with him, perhaps five years into this professional life, he was grateful to have found work as a location marshal for several London-based productions, supporting himself either through part-time work as he tried to leave behind income derived from illegal activities, even though participating in that world kept him closer to the production possibilities offered by his scene. There were also an excruciating series of practical mistakes he had made, such as only relatively recently having been introduced to Diary Services and other agencies that work around the filmmaking business, supplying labour to various projects.

From the outside, it doesn't look as if Idris's lack of success stemmed from any form of incompetence or comparative lack of expertise in a technical or aesthetic sense but simply that, unlike Nathan who himself was already bumping into the limitations of his careership, Idris had both excess and inadequacy in terms of managing external job markets outside of his participation in local scenes.

Indeed, the only person we met who was able in some ways to bridge these series of difficulties was Toma. Unlike Nathan and Idris, Toma had learned how to turn participating in projects into paid work, and in turn, he had managed to narrativise this process as a longer-term trajectory where it was perfectly plausible to describe himself as a filmmaker.

From Work to a Career

Toma had also been involved in making music videos, but, unlike Idris or Jermaine, this kind of work had become unrewarding for him because of the limitations of that form, the monotony induced by industrialised production, and ethical uncertainty on account of the legitimacy of funding sources. Like all the other three young men we have met so far, Toma's social and cultural marginal position gave him access to this world, but he soon realised that it did not offer a route to further job opportunities or even a balanced career pathway.

> I got pigeonholed as an urban music video director and after [an early success with a well-known artist] I carried on and I was just shooting loads, and loads and loads of other music videos because I understood the audience and it was a niche that I got kind of, that I trapped myself in.
>
> I wish I got into adverts. I made a few adverts, like low end adverts sort of you know, but it would be more viral stuff. It wouldn't be, like glossy TV ads that have got sort of a million pounds budget upwards. But all of that money [for music videos] was from the

record company, because we were just hired guns to go in for a day or three, shoot a music video, and then take our money and that was it. That's why I left because everybody wanted a generic music video . . . girls, strippers, boats, all of these things.

Making music videos was all encompassing; it takes up every second of your life because you're dealing with people that have massive egos. You could be making a music video for a band of four, and they're all calling you and like saying, 'what should I wear?' I'm like, 'you know we've hired a stylist; sit with the stylist.' 'Yes, but you're the director what do you think?' Dealing with some of the egos is . . . and they've got all of these egos, and at the end of it, they're just making a boring music video. You've got no life for yourself, and it's just destructive.

Toma fairly quickly realised that for all the reliability of regular income,

there's a ceiling as well; there's a glass ceiling as well, so when I was in that there were some people who had less experience in my company and weren't making music videos half as good as we were, but they must have had connections because they were moving up to the level of sort of £100,000 music videos, £250,000 music videos, and then into the millions, and I was always stuck at the sort of low end of that.

Like Nathan, Toma recognised that work didn't just mean simply exercising a skill or a single process but involved the complete execution of a project. Without the security, and without a company structure to ensure continuity in these projects, he had to adapt quickly to take control of the process of securing future work whilst continuing to complete current films successfully. Like Nathan, Toma too had a skill set that primarily revolved around DOP/camera—to use more traditional labour classifications in these industries—but usually he was involved in editing and frequently forms of writing and directing. Indeed, one key push was the desire to move away from being a subordinate on somebody else's film to controlling the whole process, which led him into both directorial and production opportunities. The problem then becomes one of financing and of learning to control the whole process of filmmaking from inception, through capitalisation, to distribution and securing returns on investment. The new digital filmmakers' control over production means that they are thrown headfirst into this larger form of competition rather than being able to find a niche where they can learn to master a discrete skill.

A considerable amount of effort thus went into work devoted to managing Toma's developing career. This took the form of securing and exploiting personal contacts; developing, curating, and promoting a portfolio; and constantly attending to an intra-personal narrative of identity that rationalised ongoing opportunities into a satisfactory story about the filmmaking-self, a process enhanced by being interviewed for this 'creative biography.' The key feature of this identity work (Oakley & O'Brien, 2016) was, it seemed to us, an emphasis on being involved in filmmaking projects, of ensuring continuing participation. As has been noted elsewhere, some of the features of creative labour enlist this sense of belonging as part of its attraction as 'good' work (Hesmondhalgh & Baker, 2011). We have already seen thus far how work is understood as a form of participation in an ongoing scene or workplace, and for Toma, securing his place in this social world revolved around how he could use specialised equipment (purchased from income on earlier projects) to play his part:

> I've got loads and loads and loads of experience shooting stuff. I've got loads of my own equipment, that's you know really good equipment, better equipment than they even had.

Intriguingly, it was how he was able to barter this knowledge and resources that ensured participation; the equipment gave his work competitive polish greater than simple 'skills.' As he noted, he'd 'never [even] been to an interview for any of the jobs that I've applied for' and, in fact, when he

> applied for like jobs in media, I never got accepted to any of them, and so I went onto the *Guardian* site and started looking at how would they do their CV different; am I not getting myself across properly in a professional context within their environment, not mine? Because in my environment, I can walk into any, I can walk in fairly comfortably into billion-pound companies and walk out with money in my pocket and a job to make a music video, but actually getting a job and transferring my skills to . . . it seemed impossible.

At one stage, Toma recounted that he took up another job as 'like financially I couldn't cope, so I had to go to the city [as a trader],' but he emphasised that 'I don't think I'd given up in the sense that, oh my God I'm never going to make a film again, forget the film industry.' Yet this was a story of continually learning from mistakes on the basis that he never lost a foothold within the by now very wide range of filmmaking circles in which he was engaged:

> I went down a different road after that. I tried something quite stupid, I tried to make a television show. I spent all the money that I earned from the city and was trying to produce this television show.

Indeed, in reviewing the interview with Toma, we discovered that there were an extraordinary range of different projects, companies, collaborations with friends, discrete commercial jobs, and longer-term project planning all going on at the same time. Unlike Nathan, Toma had no time to pay attention to aesthetic finesse but relied on a high volume of production turnover both to ensure some level of financial stability, but equally importantly to ensure that he constantly had opportunities, networks, and circuits that would allow him ongoing, continuous, and future forms of participation. When the interview began, he spent considerable energy criticising the failure of his film school to give him any practical advice in terms of making a living from how to pay taxes to the kind of business arrangements needed to operate as a freelancer—of course, this is an extremely frequent complaint—but in this case, it was clear that Toma had been on a very steep learning journey, working out so many dimensions of what he might need in order to be able to pursue this life as his career.

The Convertibility of Subcultural Capital

Two key themes running across the case studies in this book are, first, how social capital works to stratify opportunity but also how social capital is built through networks or, as we have seen, in scenes, and how that resource can be exploited and/or leveraged to build progressions across informal and formal markets for young people developing creative careers. These young men by and large do not exemplify the idea that interest-driven, digitally mediated creative practices—in this case, film—lead naturally or simply into sustained economic activity. In fact, the cases of Jermaine, Nathan, and Idris almost suggest the reverse, in that while social capital can build extraordinarily strong niche markets and clearly leads to serious income generation, it is, by definition limited, or in Toma's words, has ceilings. Secondly, these young men come from, what in the UK we would call, ethnic minorities, and in the US, non-dominant populations, whose forms of social capital are, as we have seen, rich and varied, like those in Texas and Colorado described in other chapters, but do not necessarily have currency across other social domains. The entry into music videos exemplifies both the possibilities of exploiting subcultural capital as well as its limits.

This seems to derive from the difficulties of exchanging social capital across restricted and heavily demarcated fields of activity, as Bourdieu might describe it (Bourdieu, 1990, 1993). Nathan, Jermaine, and Idris seemed to find difficulty in converting capital built up in one subcultural domain into another. To some extent, their ethnicity, and their aesthetic subfields, for varied reasons, 'pigeonholed' them. Without access to a form of careership, exemplified by Toma, which explicitly addressed the challenges of crossing these subfield boundaries, all of their experience and expertise remained trapped within their scenes—even though to a great extent, some of these scenes have quite considerable economic potential.

There is nothing especially new in the idea that social capital is an essential determinant influencing opportunity or restricting access. Similarly, understanding the power of the forms of social capital found in marginalised communities is equally well-known to sociologists, even if such an understanding is not so powerful in popular rhetoric. However, making sense of normative progressions into economic opportunity revolving around new social networks and markets disrupted by digital technologies is a still relatively under-theorised and under-researched area. The creative biographies of these young men do shed light on the uneven nature of such progressions and suggest where policy interventions might have more impact.

Conventional thinking in education tends to underplay the impact of social capital for a whole host of political reasons too numerous to list here, but one of the issues these cases raise is an overreliance on de-contextualised technique or skill as opposed to understanding how abilities—in this case filmmaking—are developed in practice and local social contexts. Secondly, developing connections between cultural scenes and informal learning institutions or initiatives seems a productive and concrete way to build pathways and opportunities that are rarely found in public education systems. Thirdly, there seems to be a need to develop forms of education that pay attention to helping young people address their identities and their careerships in the way that Toma demonstrated to us. Learning how to build contacts, how to engage in a wide number of production circuits, how to build critical mass from multiple projects rather than single linear 'jobs' are not necessarily natural or obvious or even easy-to-learn capabilities, as we will discuss in Chapter 7.

Participating in the Filmmaking Field

This chapter has sought to show how young people entering this field of work have learnt to think of entry into employment not in terms of simply 'getting a job'[but more in terms of monetising their participation in a series of fields. Scenes, stratified skills-based tasks, collaborative projects, and large-scale productions are all moving and constantly transforming ways of organising the social practice of making film in contemporary societies. From Hollywood productions, to social media, to YouTube, to television music videos, and so forth, there are a whole range of markets for filmmaking today. Digital technology has radically transformed these marketplaces but also the nature of the creative labour working in these fields. Young people entering this work now think of their skills not only in terms of conventional job distinctions but also in terms of the range of opportunities available across these marketplaces. Whether these young people are unique or, because of their more marginalised social position, in the vanguard of more widespread trends, it is difficult to say without more substantial research in this area, although our conclusions here do resonate with other findings (Allen, 2015; Ashton, 2013; Oakley & O'Brien, 2016).

It is probably stating the obvious, but the education and training routes that have grown up around film and television industries have clearly been overtaken by these changes in circumstances, and young people at the forefront of these changes have learnt quicker than their teachers what this means for them: Nelligan writes of a 'more expansive and more densely populated group of aspirants who, as 'outcasts,' construct working lives in and around the necessity to network' (Nelligan, 2015, p. 12). Although this chapter is limited to a few case studies, it seems to us that it would be extraordinarily difficult to undertake larger-scale quantitative research into these fragmented marketplaces, these changing conditions, and, indeed the huge swathe of labour working in these informal markets, precisely because of shifting definitions of occupation and company (or, in academic terms, field). The fact that these case studies are also focusing on segments of the population who consistently are underrepresented in these labour markets, yet whose creative power from 'the margins' drives innovation, only exacerbates the lack of understanding of these changes and the need for providers—both formal and informal—to come to grips with these changing opportunities.

Conceptualising entry into work as taking advantage of economic opportunity or as a mode of participation is going to be a difficult challenge for policymakers for either education or industrial strategy. However, it seems to be the only way we can find to explain how these young people imagined, planned, and built careers. In some respects, the dimensions of participation that we have encountered in this chapter can be represented diagrammatically (see Figure 4.1), although that doesn't quite capture elements of recursion, social circuits and flow of the interruptions, false starts, and disconnects that are clearly part of what it means to work as a filmmaker today.

These barriers are partly the result of an oversupply of labour, but they also show how the field of filmmaking itself is continuously being restructured and reorganised. In some respects, the elements of this diagram are quite traditional; there is nothing new about exploiting contacts, the need for formal training, the role of peers, and so forth. Whilst the new importance of careership, as described in this chapter, cannot be understated and seems absolutely central to unlocking any form of continuing participation, it is how this diagram represents work as participation in and across subfields that sheds new light on the changing meaning of filmmaking. We need to attend to the ways that young people are redefining the nature and meaning of such creative labour as they apply models of their social worlds to fast-changing opportunities in the digital age.

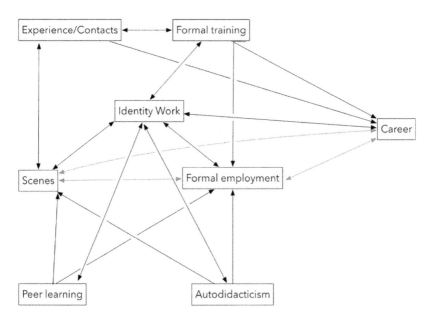

Figure 4.1 Diagram Showing the Elements of Participation in the Field of Filmmaking

Notes

1. For older studies of the relationship between (class) identity and work see Sennett and Cobb (1973).
2. There are self-evident limitations in this data set, but the intention was to use emic perspectives to begin to theorise the field. Although the interviewees were both men and women, the chapter does not address questions of gender. For studies of creative labour in this respect, see Huws (2007), Gill (2009), Kennedy (2011).

References

Allen, M. (2015). *'Hard labour': Young people moving into work in difficult times*. London, UK: Radical Education.

Ashton, D. (2013). Cultural workers in-the-making. *European Journal of Cultural Studies, 16*(4), 468–488.

Ashton, D. (2014). Creative contexts: Work placement subjectivities for the creative industries. *British Journal of Sociology of Education, 37*(2), 1–20.

Ashton, D. (2015). Making media workers: Contesting film and television industry career pathways. *Television & New Media, 16*(3), 275–294.

Baldwin, R. (2016). *The great convergence: Information technology and the new globalization*. Cambridge, MA: Harvard University Press.

Banks, M., & Oakley, K. (2015). The dance goes on forever? Art schools, class and UK higher education. *International Journal of Cultural Policy, 22*(1), 1–17.

Bourdieu, P. (1990). *The logic of practice*. Cambridge, UK: Polity Press.

Bourdieu, P. (1993). *The field of cultural production: Essays on art and literature*. Cambridge, UK: Polity Press.

Caldwell, J. T. (2008). *Production culture: Industrial reflexivity and critical practice in film and television*. Durham, NC: Duke University Press Books.

Caves, R. E. (2000). *Creative industries: Contracts between art and commerce*. Boston, MA: Harvard University Press.

Furlong, A., & Cartmel, F. (2006). *Young people and social change: New perspectives* (2nd ed.). Milton Keynes, UK: Open University Press.

Gill, R. (2009). Creative biographies in new media: Social innovation in Web work. In P. Jeffcutt & A. Pratt (Eds.), *Creativity and innovation* (pp. 161–178). London, UK: Routledge.

Guile, D. (2006). Access, learning and development in the creative and cultural sectors: From "creative apprenticeship" to "being apprenticed." *Journal of Education and Work*, 19(5), 433–453.

Hesmondhalgh, D., & Baker, S. (2011). *Creative labour: Media work in three cultural industries*. Culture, economy and the social series. London, UK: Routledge.

Hodkinson, P. (2008). *Understanding career decision-making and progression: Careership revisited*. Proceedings from John Killen Memorial Lecture, London, UK.

Hodkinson, P., & Sparkes, A. C. (1997). Careership: A sociological theory of career decision making. *British Journal of Sociology of Education*, 18(1), 29–44.

Huws, U. (2007). *The spark in the engine: Creative work in the new economy*. London, UK: The Merlin Press Ltd.

Ito, M., Baumer, S., Bittanti, M., boyd, d., Cody, R., Herr-Stephenson, B. . . . Tripp, L. (2010). *Hanging out, messing around, and geeking out: Kids living and learning with new media*. Boston, MA: The MIT Press.

Kennedy, H. (2011). *Network: Ethics and values in web design*. New York, NY: Palgrave.

Lobato, R., Thomas, J., & Hunter, D. (2011). Histories of user-generated content: Between formal and informal media economies. *International Journal of Communication*, 5, 899–914.

Mayer, V., Banks, M. J., & Caldwell, J. T. (2009). *Production studies: Cultural studies of media industries* (1st ed.). New York, NY: Routledge.

Morgan, G., Wood, J., & Nelligan, P. (2013). Beyond the vocational fragments: Creative work, precarious labour and the idea of "flexploitation." *The Economic and Labour Relations Review*, 24(3), 397–415.

Nelligan, P. (2015). No guarantees: Preparing for long-term precarious employment in the Australian film and television industry. *Social Alternatives*, 34(4), 22–27.

Oakley, K., & O'Brien, D. (2016). Learning to labour unequally: Understanding the relationship between cultural production, cultural consumption and inequality. *Social Identities*, 22(5), 1–16.

O'Brien, D., Laurison, D., Miles, A., & Friedman, S. (2016). Are the creative industries meritocratic? An analysis of the 2014 British Labour Force Survey. *Cultural Trends*, 25(2), 116–131.

Peiperl, M. A., Arthur, M. B., & Anand, N. (2002). *Career creativity: Explorations in the remaking of work*. Oxford, UK: Oxford University Press.

Peters, M. A., & Bulut, E. (Eds.). (2011). *Cognitive capitalism, education and digital labor* (1st new ed.). New York, NY: Peter Lang Publishing Inc.

Sefton-Green, J. (2017). WAC arts. In K. Peppler (Ed.), *The SAGE encyclopaedia of out-of-school learning* (pp. 823–826). Thousand Oaks, CA: Sage Publications.

Sennett, R., & Cobb, J. (1973). *The hidden injuries of class.* New York, NY: Vintage.

Srnicek, N., & Williams, A. (2016). *Inventing the future: Postcapitalism and a world without work* (Revised and updated ed.). London, UK: Verso.

Standing, G. (2016). *The precariat: The new dangerous class* (Bloomsbury Revelations ed.). London, UK: Bloomsbury Academic.

Straw, W. (1991). Systems of articulation, logics of change: communities and scenes in popular music. *Cultural Studies, 5*(3), 368–388.

Terranova, T. (2004). *Network culture: Politics for the information age.* London, UK: Pluto Press.

Woo, B., Rennie, J., & Poyntz, S. (2014). Scene thinking. *Cultural Studies, 29*(3), 285–297.

5 Engaging Youth in Industry-Led Filmmaking Projects

The Limits of Social and Cultural Capital in Career Making

Julian Sefton-Green

Introduction

The chapter is built around a set of interviews with young people who attended the early years of a course run by the British Film Institute (BFI) in England, known as the Film Academy.[1] The course was set up to address a particular set of concerns around the non-representativeness of the creative labour force. Despite the fact that competition for jobs in the creative and cultural industries—especially in film or TV production—is intense and despite the fact that there is a huge pool of reserve labour often 'between jobs,' there is still significant political (and in the UK, at any rate, policy) interest in developing opportunities and access for young people in these employment fields. Looked at objectively, this might seem slightly illogical: why should any investment or interest be paid to contribute to the oversupply of labour in the creative industries? However, for a range of reasons, the creative and cultural industries are an important touchstone in debates about equality, fairness, access, and opportunity.

The key sensitivity surrounds the lack of equal or fair representation in film and TV both on-screen and behind it (the production crew) in terms of social class, gender, and/or race. The recent furore around the 2016 Oscar ceremony with the Twitter storm #oscarsSoWhite and the persistent anger around the data produced showing the raw statistics behind the gendered and racial composition of the creative labour force in both the UK and the US[2] all point to the continuing importance of this issue. In public debate, there is an assumed relationship between the social composition of film and programme makers and the nature of media output. Although rarely spelled out, the presumption is that the social representativeness of the creative labour force will have a direct effect on the media they make and produce. Whilst, in public debate at least, this dynamic is rarely contextualised in a more widespread discussion about racial and gendered power relations—reducing questions about structural inequality in society to the effects of individual actions—it does try to hold to account how media corporations recruit and sustain their labour forces and even influence which projects to fund. A further theorisation of the relationship between the social composition of the creative workforce and media output has focused on the relationship between media consumption and media production (Oakley & O'Brien, 2016) in trying to interrogate more deeply what's at stake in our current interest in the representativeness of the creative labour force. In the UK, this often takes the form of repeated anxieties, as in the BBC director-general's comment about the 'hideously white BBC' of 2001, which was then resurrected in 2014, given failure to address any of these kinds of questions at a systemic and structural level.

One common argument across this array of debates, anxiety, defensiveness, and both good and bad will, is the concern with talent. Again, talent itself is assumed to be an innate quality residing in an individual (as opposed to other conceptualisations of creativity being produced in social situations). Repeatedly, the argument of justifying the current composition of the creative labour force is the meritocratic rationale of talent: that initiatives aimed at ameliorating unfair representation can block a natural supply of ability, thus inhibiting competitiveness. The argument about the oversupply of labour is often rejected on the basis that people just aren't good enough—that the need for exceptional talent justifies an asymmetric labour market.

Responses to the concerns about the skewed composition of the labour force frequently take the form of initiatives or projects, often situated outside of the formal education system, such as in school holidays, and over a short period of time, targeting young people from less privileged backgrounds (the definition of which is a constant source of concern) and often funded by high-profile government (in the UK) and/or philanthropic or media industries. Although employment is mainly a relevant issue to people in their 20s at least, another key assumption is that there are 'downstream' blockages so that the early identification and recruitment of potential talent needs to take place prior to the age when young people might be competing for work itself. These projects and initiatives often blend together a range of aims, from simply inspiring youth to creating social networks, to creating high-quality introductory activities bringing together industry personnel and young people themselves in a belief that such projects can in some way help solve the desires, ambitions, and political interests in what is perceived to be an important barrier to creating a better or fairer media production ecology.

There is no simple way to characterise the logic of these assumptions, but their inconsistencies, prejudices, and high-stakes visibility lie behind the young people's experiences of training and career building reported in this chapter. The project which led to the interviews stemmed from precisely the kinds of concerns outlined earlier: a concern that the creative labour force was being drawn from an exclusive minority, a desire to develop a more diverse filmmaking workforce, and the desire to develop all talents. Whilst this may have been the rationale for the development of the initiative, this is not to say that such a concern directly influenced the young people who applied for places in this course. Indeed, the chapter is not so much concerned with the supplier side of the argument; it does not disentangle the motives or indeed the impact metrics employed by the initiative to account for its success. It is not intended to evaluate the success of the intervention. Instead, the chapter focuses on the ways that young people took up and interpreted the trajectory of becoming a filmmaker—not just suggested by participating in this course, but how these sorts of opportunities intersected with other ways of imagining a creative career discussed in this book.

The BFI, like the providers of similar kinds of interventions, formulated this particular project to support a specific kind of career trajectory and, therefore, intended the intervention to recruit young people who might not normally consider that pathway into it. However, as other chapters in this volume make clear, the notion of making film, or art, or music as a career cannot really be modelled on the forms of vocational preparation institutionalised by school or college. The customary pathways, routes, and accreditation requirements into film aren't orthodox in the same way as those required to become a lawyer or a doctor. The young people who were interested in becoming filmmakers and who chose to participate in this programme understood this, and the chapter aims to examine how they interpreted the offer to 'become' filmmakers in the light of contradictory and constantly changing information about how to plan for the unplannable, to aspire to the extraordinarily difficult, and to chart a career through muddy and unclear waters.

From Careership to Future-Making

Conventionally, the term 'career' is used to refer to linear progression through a hierarchy of related jobs within a settled professional environment. However, now that few people stay with one firm for the whole of their working lives, this definition no longer necessarily holds (Moore, Gunz, & Hall, 2007). As individuals move between organisations and adopt different working practices, it has become necessary to reframe older notions of 'experience, position, role, or activity' (Gunz, Mayrhofer, & Tolbert, 2011) within a much wider understanding of the relationship between individuals, organisations, and social context. A 'career' is increasingly understood to be both objective and subjective: it is determined by the external circumstances of employment opportunities whilst simultaneously forged and narrated by individuals (Mathieu, 2012): careers 'are creative endeavours in themselves' (Anand, Peiperl, & Arthur, 2002, p. 5). In this context, any initiative recruiting young people into film as a career has to be multifaceted.

For example, a key concept emerging from the literature capturing the changing pattern of working life is the idea of a 'boundaryless' or 'disorderly' career—a trajectory forged by the individual rather than a by an institution (Peiperl, Arthur, & Anand, 2002). As outlined in this book's introduction, this is a key feature of work in the creative industries, and it raises a number of questions about a young person's understanding of, and preparedness for, career management, career progression in professions where there is no obvious career ladder (such as film), time-intense and/or contract-based employment, and forms of recognition and status credentials derived from achievements and portfolios (as opposed to titles and pay grades) (see Mathieu, 2012).

The general implication that emerges from the literature is the need for a serious and informed preparatory understanding about the changing nature of work, without which young people entering the creative industries are likely to face confusion and unfulfilled expectations. A sociological explanation for career decision making suggests that we do not make open-ended existential choices about the future at all, but we make decisions within 'horizons for action' (Hodkinson & Sparkes, 1997). This concept suggests that it is more helpful to think about how individuals frame the implications of what they do or do not decide to do in terms of a) how they understand the opportunity structures of the labour market and b) what skills or forms of accreditation come to seem important to them. Expectations, upbringing, and social class will determine the ways young people reach these understandings.

Conventional research into the career decision-making process tends to look backwards and/or longitudinally, and rarely takes a tracking or shadowing approach to look at how young people might get drawn to particular fields of endeavour (Sefton-Green & Brown, 2014). In the literature examining 'careership,' scholars talk about concepts like 'transformations, epiphanies, routines and turning points' (Hodkinson, 2008) as narrative devices people use to account for the flow of life, taking into account happenstance and serendipity, as well as *post hoc* rationalisation. Even at this embryonic stage of their careers, this chapter suggests that young people draw on these kinds of explanations to explain or justify decisions.

The message that emerges from the literature on career pathways is that terms such as 'choosing' and 'deciding' often misrepresent the nature of the navigational process (Ball, Maguire, & Macrae, 2000). We need, instead, to look more closely at the more irrational and intangible aspects of identity formation. How do young people develop a sense of what they are good at? How do they develop a sense of their own agency and autonomy? How does this shape the ways in which they come to imagine their future selves and future careers?

In a rare study of young (prospective) creatives, Gilje and Groeng explored young filmmakers, looking at how they talked about genre and how they communicated with each other to establish their identities as professional equals (Gilje & Groeng, 2015). This attention to the mechanisms which young people use to identify themselves as prospective creators, which can include questions about confidence, self-presentation and the capacity to imagine themselves as actors within the professional field, offers fruitful ways to look at the young digital creatives.

The term 'future-making' might help explain and theorise an ongoing process of alignment, negotiation, and renegotiation that preoccupies young people and their families right from when they begin formal education (Erstad, Gilje, Sefton-Green, & Arnseth, 2016, Ch. 6). This term emphasises the agency and work done by the young person and his/her family in actively imagining and trying to map out realistic next steps. Indeed, as this chapter argues, it is impossible to separate family and school expectations of the purposes of education from this more personal process of future-making. People clearly calculate and recalculate potentials and possibilities, and more long-standing narratives about projected identities clearly play a determining part in some young people's lives, however neutrally the local context appears to offer futures for all.

Erstad et al. (2016) expanded Keri Facer's notion of 'future-making' (Facer, 2011) to look beyond simple notions of educational qualifications and making a living towards focusing on how young people negotiate possibilities and options for themselves in their personal trajectories. As indicated in our stories in this chapter, an individual's future-making is frequently bound up with family and other adult expectations that the individual has to moderate, accept, or reject as he or she creates his or her own path. However, the path for film is opaque.

Narratives of Individual and Collective 'Skills'

This opacity led to a number of critical differences in emphasis between the young people's experience of the Film Academy programme and the organisers of it. Film, of course, is an intensely social creative process; it requires significant collective teamwork, the coordination of individual roles towards common goals, and, of course, the mastery and control of a wide range of technological processes. These processes have become codified as assets of technical functions: sound, photography, staging, directing, and so on. This socio-technological system is not easy to reconcile with an individualistic conception of innate talent. The attention to individual examination performance within the formal school system does not always translate into an ability to work with others and to play a discrete part in a collective production. School's emphasis on individual attainment also means that young people themselves tend to focus on their individual accomplishments as a way of making sense of their progress rather than on other ways of reflecting on participation in a group effort. This outlook also affected the processes of selection and the kind of claims made by the young people at the application stage for these programmes. As interviewees described their work, they tended to account for their own individual performances as a way of measuring collective success, so dominant were school-based metrics of defining achievement.

For example, Bill, like many of the other interviewees, recounted experiences of making films as quite a small child:

> When I was about 7-ish, I remember he was saying, 'Ooh, like, ah, films are really cool,' and I remember thinking, really? They're not that cool. And then, I think it was on holiday in Florida, when I, I think I was 8, and my dad gave me, because he was getting a new camera, and he gave me his old big clunky tape one, and said, 'Here you go, Bill. You can have this; make films with it.' And so I did, and it was, it was really good fun. And from then on, I was filming.

We shall return to the issue of resource-rich social backgrounds later in the chapter, but this autobiography of filmmaking as a vocation—something which grabbed interest and reinforced a narrative of talent and interest, and thus being special—was common across all these interviewees (suggesting, of course, then that it was this kind of narrative which both secured them access to the programme and/or which the programme itself reinforced as a model of latent capability). Bea, here, has a similar story of origin:

> My dad's a head teacher, so I had really long summer holidays in comparison to him, so I started just. . . . I would go to his school for a week just to, kind of, help out and . . . or I'd read in the library, and he realised that I was quite interested in cameras and computers, and he realised that . . . because I went on some sort of course when I was, like, really young, I could use iMovie, and so he started getting me to film kids and to edit it, and he'd play it at parent evenings and his school assemblies and stuff.

In both of these cases, filmmaking is a form of authorial voice, of individual control and expressivity, yet professional filmmaking of the sort that the programme wanted to introduce to these young people is the opposite, with its emphasis on technical expertise and role differentiation. Both Bill and Bea had understood this and had created a developmental narrative where the authorial interest progresses into specialised expertise. As Bill, reflecting a few years back, explained,

> That would be in Year 10, a couple of years ago. And, I think it was because in drama, we were doing a kind of practical thing, a controlled assessment, and we had to either choose to do a technical thing, or acting, for it. We were like in groups, and stuff. So, I decided, because I'd always been interested in lighting, I decided, great, I'm going to do technical. My teacher said to me, 'well why don't you try out sound, and then do lighting for a different one, so you get a bit of a mixture.' So, I was like okay, I tried it out, and I discovered that

actually, there's a lot more to it than people think, and I realised I was quite good at it, and I thought this is, it's quite good fun. I thought, this could be what I maybe want to do.

All the young people in this sample told stories of 'epiphanies,' to use Hodkinson's (2008) term, suggesting a form of being chosen, of stumbling into an art form that then steers their future course. As Alan put it, 'Like a lot of young filmmakers, when I read about their autobiographies, they always talk about how they had a Super 8 when they were a child and everything.' This type of vocation—of being called—manifests itself in a wide range of participation. For example, after the initial work for her father, Bea then detailed a series of experiences and projects that showed a continuous involvement in filmmaking activities: by the same token, Bill's interest in lighting was proceeded by a series of drama experiences. It is significant that both young people's experiences are defined as meaningful precisely because they don't simply take place in school and knit together the vocation as something which takes place in leisure time, implying a greater sense of personal commitment. It is equally significant that these narratives of career identity—or early expressions of 'careership' to use the language from earlier—also are framed by the opportunities provided for these young people rather than, as they tell the stories, made *by* them. In other words, if participating in these experiences adds up to a narrative of vocation, being able to do so is a prerequisite, but is rarely seen by the young people themselves in terms of the advantageous social capital that it might represent to an outsider.

The tension between a narrative of vocation which emphasises individual control and, in reality, means a form of total auteurship—a form of filmmaking only really made possible by digital technology[3]—and participating through a specific role, as in Bill's case being interested in lighting, is worthwhile teasing out because it identifies a distinctive form of talent. The capacity to demonstrate interest and especially purpose and drive through the desire to participate suggests a valuing of self-direction rather than the performance of expertise. Yet Bea and Bill acknowledge the role of their families in transporting them to all of their various extracurricular activities, even if they don't recognise how lucky they were to attend schools with these experiences on offer. Whereas the young people, no doubt influenced by how attainment is defined at school, construct a narrative that stresses self-composure, motivation, and drive, participation in these collective activities is successful precisely because of the capacity to collaborate rather than compete individually.

Yet none of the young people had access to a specialised language or a metric of participation that could acknowledge this dimension of talent except in terms of emotional or social pleasure. As Bea put it,

And that was insane, just having someone to do every job, and you're just doing one job, and you really get to focus on being a cinematographer, because on my . . . on my regional academy [the precursor to the intensive course], I was director, writer, and director of photography, and it was really great just being able to focus on being a cinematographer. . . . I'd never really worked with a director before. Having that director-cinematographer, kind of, relationship that's so key to making films and getting to experience that, that was amazing.

Rather than describing the creative process in terms of job differentiation and specialisation, here the process is translated into affective experience.

From Social Experiences to Social Production

Indeed, the emphasis on pleasure and enjoyment confused the deliverers of this program. Whilst it was important that the young people were motivated and engaged, it seemed puzzling to them that reflections on the programme focused on the emotional quality of the experience. At one stage, this led to some amusement between the deliverers and the evaluators when it became clear that survey responses showed that attending the programme was mainly valued because of the people they had met: it seemed an inappropriate use of public funds to act as an introductions agency.

However, this attention to sociality may not quite have meant what the deliverers thought it did and, in fact, stands as a proxy for a way of talking about important, yet rarely articulated, learning processes. Jess may have said that she

> made many friends. They're all so lovely because I think they didn't . . . none of them realised I was 16. It was only just one evening, actually, maybe a day or two in, everyone was saying, oh, so where are you from, and I was like, well, I'm still doing GCSEs, and they just didn't believe me. And then when they knew, they, kind of, I guess at some points they looked after me, which I didn't need looking after, but it was nice.

It would be a mistake, however, just to read these kinds of responses solely in terms of affect. Although rudimentary and untheorised, participants did have some sense of how the medium of film required collaboration to move forward. Here is Bea again:

> I like being with other people. I really like collaborating. I really like that kind of . . . just having something to bounce off, because I . . . like, I was always making documentaries or making little animations that had no story, and I don't think I'm good at coming up with the entire thing. I think I need someone to bounce off, and I've realised that more and more growing up: I need someone with me.

The difficulty, as suggested by the earlier section, is that the dominant languages of teaching and learning are themselves fairly unsophisticated when it comes to isolating the features of collaboration which are central to large-scale production activities. Jack is perhaps more de-centred than Bea and analyses creative production more in terms of role functions than friendship when describing the making process in terms of

> [t]he seriousness and the maturity and the, kind of, being indepen-dent because you don't rely on friends because they're not there and you are, kind of, given your role and expected to do it, obviously being taught beforehand, and it's just it . . . yes, it was the indepen-dence that was exciting.

This was a rare discursive move away from a language of friendship and affect to a search for terms that could give insight into the collaborative process. Nevertheless, the dominant attention to individual performance and the fact that this was effectively a competitive programme drawing on forms of selection tended to frame ability more in individual terms than in any fully fledged attention to what collaboration could mean in practice.

Working with other people does, of course, rely on shared norms and assumptions and ways of behaving that are very difficult to disentan-gle from social class. Indeed, many of the comments about their peers stressed like-mindedness or forms of mutual understanding around genre that bore out previous research around bonding through shared aesthet-ics (Gilje & Groeng, 2015). As Jack put it,

> I learnt a lot, made some friends up there. For me, because at that time I was really dedicated to documentary, that was what I really wanted to do, and it was all documentary for that so it, sort of, floated my boat completely.

Like many programmes, attendance and participation is voluntary, but such volition doesn't just indicate individual motivation or drive; it's also a sorting mechanism to enable young people to find and recognise their peers. Indeed, programmes dedicated to supporting creative production need to focus on this recognition, or even understand it as a form of social attraction, in order to allow for the kinds of understandings about role and teamwork that we have just seen. For these interviewees, again, there was a linguistic deficit in the recognition process. Alan, for example, describes the process as follows:

> It was meeting all the like-minded people that were actually as reli-able. It was like the reliable filmmakers I wanted to know in college. Unfortunately, they still live quite far away.

Reliability may not even be the right word, even if it is not just a question of practical logistics. Jack can see that like-mindedness is a form of creative opportunity:

> Because we're all, like, still talking even after the [course] and a few of them have already met up. A few of them I think have even made a film with each other already, but I just don't have that luck at the moment.

This kind of sentiment may be expressed in the rather generalised language of affect—and we are suggesting that the quality of this discourse is a reflection of the wider culture rather than anything individual—but time and time again, these participants echoed Jess's positive evaluation of the experience:

> And then just the experience of being with like-minded people for such a long time who were all interested in film. I had, like, a lot of time that I could just talk to them all and work with them, [it] was really nice.

Whilst the programme suppliers may have misread these kinds of attachments, we want to suggest that the young people themselves were using the experience of these programmes to sort and find like-minded types. This is not just a form of class-based social recognition, although undoubtedly such factors were at work, but actually showed that the young people understood that making film was a highly complex social process and that they were picking up the need to interact with others, create teams, and build cadres of like-minded 'friends' (we might say colleagues, even if that word might not suggest sufficient emotional intensity [Gregg, 2011]). They were demonstrating sophisticated future-oriented understandings of the kind of behaviours that might serve them if their careers progressed. The extent to which this form of group bonding represents the learning of a particular kind of social capital is the subject of the next section.

From Planning a Career to Leveraging Social Capital

Participating in this course, as in many arts education activities, encouraged the development of expressions of aesthetic taste, in this instance, it was around film or filmmakers. In interviews, both Bea and Bill expressly made the point that they liked the work of Edgar Wright, and Jack name-checked Roger Deakins, reflecting the teaching they had experienced. Part of the work these kinds of courses, and indeed education more generally, is to expose young people to different kinds of art, but also to encourage students to nominate membership of taste communities

(Bourdieu, 1984). This course supported the shared appreciation of taste judgements. Making visible these affinities through these kinds of comments was an important way for the young people to mark the journey they were travelling. They 'performed' expertise through their identity claims, reinforcing the kinds of community values promulgated by the course as part of the narrative of careership.

The exposure to different kinds of aesthetics and the attempts to belong to these taste communities demonstrates the acquisition of distinctive forms of cultural capital (Savage, 2015). Cultural capital describes the acquisition of forms of aesthetic judgement and cultural knowledge that distinguishes social groups from one another. It is intimately related to the acquisition of social capital which is the connection to other people who might have the capacity to help materially support or assist with career development. An explicit aim of this course was to introduce young participants to the established world of filmmaking through both regional and then national workshops where well-known and active professionals would be available to the young people. Whilst the more 'famous' speakers may not in themselves have been in the position to provide contact or direct support, the workshops were also filled with a range of working professionals at various stages of their careers who were, of course, networked into the industry and who themselves would then be able to act as points of contact and facilitate further introductions for the students. Thus, in addition to building up networks of peers as part of the social capital that might support career building as described in the previous section, participants learnt the value of making connections with professionals to understand how forms of networking might help capitalise forms of future-making. This is both personally challenging (being shy or unconfident is an active hindrance here) and conceptually different from the notion of attainment found in everyday schooling (it is a form of behaviour that hangs on understanding the rules of an implicit and often un-stated game).

Valerie, (who was interviewed for Chapter 4 as a young filmmaker but who earlier in her life participated in BFI projects), describes how she learnt this process when she was exposed to a wider audience for a documentary she made initially at school:

> But we were also invited to do, to network, a networking event. I think we were told by the Media Trust or Limelight or one of those organisations, and it was a networking event for people from the industry and young people who were kind of like wanting to get into the industry. And from that event, I met two people, and like even though I'm proactive, I'm also shy, so I said to one of my friends who knew I wanted to meet her, but I wouldn't network with anyone else, she was staying round the corner, and she was like 'Valerie you can't do this if you want to network, if you want to be in this industry.'

So she dragged me to one random guy that she'd picked, and she was like, 'hi, my friend wants to be in the media industry,' and from that moment onwards I started talking to that guy, and now he's on my board. . . . His name is P. He, like, he has a sense of history, he's worked for the BBC, he's created one of the departments in the BBC, over in Ireland I think where he came from, he went over and worked with Discovery in America, he now goes to oversee production companies for CTTV, so he's got like a wealth of experience.

The subsequent history of Valerie's career showed the value of these kinds of contacts and how she had learnt to exploit them both to envisage and build a professional identity and life for herself. Paradoxically, although the programme discussed in this chapter was explicit about developing contacts and teaching aspiring professionals the value of them in exactly the ways that the authors of a recent article on the value of what they called 'brokering' in youth programmes advocate (Ching, Santo, Hoadley, & Peppler, 2016), it didn't quite have the same kind of effect as we have just seen with Valerie.

The young people in this course saw the development of social capital much more in terms of peer relationships and immediate resources, as Ed put it when discussing next steps:

So yes, I think, I'm not entirely sure whether I'll apply [to university] at the end of this year, or the next year, for schools, but I've, I'm quite lucky, in that, again, the sense that I networked whilst working on the feature film. And so, I've got things like my own short films, that I want to create, but I've also networked with people on there, that hopefully I may be able to get onto another feature film at the end of this year, that the costume designer was organising, and then, their props master had another project, which he was happy to get me involved with, so I've kind of got things that are professional projects, that I get involved with, as well as my own personal ones.

There is a clear sense of learning how to exploit the experience, but it is also perhaps limited. The frame for future growth, for future-making, and the proposed career trajectory remains slightly underdeveloped in terms of personal creative work. This contrasts with Valerie's example earlier (even though she was the same age as Ed) in terms of the capability to leverage contacts and networks to enter into a different level of work.

This might suggest that a principle of brokering, and an attention to the social capital benefits of networking, may need more subtle interpretation: see Chapter 8. Jess certainly noted about the programme that 'it was something to do with film that looked really good, and with the BFI, it sounded serious and it sounded official, so it sounded like something that would really benefit me.' However, as we have just seen with Ed, calibrating this ambition requires a different kind of careership. Indeed, many of the young people saw the networking opportunities much more in terms of learning how to navigate future courses in places of learning. Thus, for example, Allie made sense of her contact with professionals more in terms of skill development than network opportunities:

> [I] sat in front of a locations manager who, she worked on *Under the Skin*, and, like, quite big productions. And used to just have these big chats with her about production in general, and was just really inspired by her, actually. And she really, she would point out the mistakes we were making and, you know, and just, I think, yes, it was, it was really great just to sit and have that chat to her almost every day, you know?

And far more common were explanations about future career choices structured in terms of formal navigation through different institutions than the capacity to utilise the networking opportunities that apparently were placed in front of them. Jack's imagined career trajectory here is typical in its level of planning in detail and its markers in terms of institutional accreditation:

> From now, right, so it's going to be Ravensbourne three years. From talking to people that I've talked to there, I'm going to hopefully get some work experience. Well, not work experience, I'm going to get work, part-time, doing some filming stuff, being a runner, because they're things I like doing. Then after that I'll probably, like, a few years maybe of doing corporate work and DP-ing some indie films. Then I want to go to National Film Television School, do the cinematography course there. Come out of there, go straight into being a DP on something higher up. Move my way up, and then I'll be the biggest DP, that's it.

Ironically, many of the tutors on the programme were of the generation when entry into film did not require university-level accreditation or indeed formal apprenticeship but took place at a time when employment was more fluid and open. These tutors were actually quite sceptical about the value of higher education courses, suggesting that building a portfolio, perhaps in the way that Ed has just described earlier, is the way forward. This kind of attitude is quite common in the industry and, of course, only reinforces disparities in social capital. Whilst Valerie's entry into film had been 'brokered' through networking, introductions, and contacts, and her whole career had taken place precisely within the framework of studying media studies and film in pursuing both formal and informal courses, we also met Simon, who had actually been advised by his teachers not to study film or media at university and solely to concentrate on building up his portfolio in exploiting his considerable access to various forms of social and/or cultural capital.

The fact that most of the young people we interviewed were only focusing on the best educational route to success in the face of this 'university of life' advice is instructive and shows the limits of an attention to brokering as an explicit aim of these kinds of intervention programmes. Yet from the young person's point of view, focusing on university, and the kind of pathway planning that they were used to (and which of course, keeps options open), is the more rational choice. As suggested in the discussion about individual versus collective skills, or, indeed, in the restricted repertoire available to these young people to describe like-mindedness, simply offering a superficial engagement with certain kinds of behaviours (forms of social capital) just could not be taken up by these young people. At this stage in their lives, they approached this course far more influenced by the ways that attainment, career progression, and future steps had been laid out *for* them rather than being open to the kinds of language, values, and professional outlooks that were on offer in the BFI curriculum. From this perspective, it appears as if these kinds of programmes and interventions, however well-intentioned and however well-structured and organised, are going to be limited in the ways that they impact the kinds of careership or future-making that young people, at this point in time, demonstrated through their interpretations of this course.

Conclusion: Careership as Re-contextualisation and the Irony of Policy Responses

This chapter has effectively suggested that participating in this course enabled these young people to practice new modes of careership, introducing them to ways of imagining, marking, and negotiating their futures in ways that the rationale for the course, with its focus on introducing professional filmmaking practices, was unprepared for. There were clearly disjunctions between the broader aspirations behind this kind of provision and the ways that it's take-up in action was interpreted and used by the young people themselves. This is perhaps not unsurprising—perhaps even foreseeable—but what does it tell us about the ways that young people themselves might navigate pathways into employment and negotiate entry into the creative industries?

Kate and Oakley and Dave O'Brien identified a dearth of research addressing the causal connections 'between who works in the production of culture, what cultural forms this labour force produces, how the consumption of these forms are stratified and what difference this makes to the replication, reinforcement or reduction of social inequality' (Oakley & O'Brien, 2016, p. 11), and to an extent, our argument here is a response to this challenge.

The chapter has explored the contradictory relationship between the school examination system that identifies individual performance and a creative filmmaking culture that emphasises collegiality and collaboration, arguing that the young people themselves focused on forms of identity validation through peer recognition and the development of cultural capital. However, explicit attempts to leverage social capital actually ended up being re-contextualised by the mode of career privileged by schooling (with its emphasis on high-stakes, high-status institutional validation) rather than perhaps the more informal experiential learning preferred by the creative industries. Oakley and O'Brien have noted the attention to 'a particular sort of self-identity' (2016, p. 8) in higher education selection processes and how this is inextricably related to social class:

> Self-cultivation is a life-long process of 'playing the game,' beginning with the bewildering variety of extra school activities undertaken by some middle-class children in childhood, an undertaking used to develop competitive advantage for the labor market.
> (Oakley & O'Brien, 2016, p. 8)

Our program's interest in finding and developing talent cannot escape this process, and we have seen how the young people's understanding of what talent might actually consist of, and how it can be imagined and described, has taken the form of self-cultivation as it has made sense to a generation continuously being directed towards competitive examination performance. This may lead to a situation where the initiatives aiming to challenge structural inequalities only end up reinforcing their norms and practices. Again, this is a familiar outcome exemplifying a continuing and ongoing struggle when legislating for equality in an historically unequal competitive social context.

These broader political implications are perhaps towards the edges of the frame of this book. There are other less broad but equally useful implications from this study, in particular those relating to the implications for initiatives that try to redistribute social capital. One suggestion about the fact that for these young people, social capital consisted of a strengthening of peer bonding rather than knowing how to exploit industry contacts, is that it indicates a developmental progression in the process of future-making. That is, until these young people are in the position of acting independently in the labour marketplace, their instincts and their cultivation orientate them towards a more risk-adverse focus on formal institutional accreditation. After all, they know, even if their tutors wanted to ignore the fact, that labour-market saturation in the creative industries now means that formal accreditation plays an increasingly important sorting role in ensuring access to that market. This may suggest that future programmes could pay attention to how 'self-cultivation' is managed, along with an explicit attention to the issue of membership of diverse taste cultures, and how forms of 'like-mindedness' are sustained, managed, and developed in order to build more effective links with the ambitions and aspirations young people will bring with them to participation.

Secondly, there is the suggestion that different ways of talking about relationships, and especially those which affect collaboration, need strengthening and formalising. The preponderance of narratives which began with authorial enthusiasm rather than technical interest, and an attention to different forms of role specialisation, are also ways of identifying and analysing what it is to be creative in practice and what talent actually means 'on the job.' Here young people need access to different horizons to manage labour-market opportunities in different ways of talking about individual performance in these contexts. Again, this has implications for the ways in which young people are currently encouraged to assess themselves through academic performance and its limited utility in transferring into the filmmaking domain. A change of terminology with different metrics for evaluation might also impact the class-based interest in self-cultivation—which only perpetuates the forms of selection and stratification—that policy-based interventions are ambitious to change.

Notes

1. www.bfi.org.uk/education-research/5-19-film-education-scheme-2013-2017/bfi-film-academy-scheme. The scheme operated at both regional and national levels, inviting young people in their final years at school to apply and then be selected for extended and even residential filmmaking courses run by professionals with the aim of offering excluded and marginalised social groups high-level professionalised filmmaking opportunities.

    For the purposes of research, the author was involved in the external evaluation of the programme and additionally interviewed the programme facilitators and eight participants towards the end of their participation, reviewing their motives for becoming involved and their future plans and aspirations to work in film. Projects completed during the programme and other outcomes from the teaching process also fed into this work. Interviews conducted for Chapter 7 where some of the young filmmakers reflected on their participation in these kinds of programmes were also used here.
2. www.theguardian.com/film/2017/sep/20/british-cinema-gender-imbalance-worse-2017-bfi-filmography, based on https://filmography.bfi.org.uk and www.hollywoodreporter.com/news/usc-study-diversity-movies-largely-unchanged-increased-awareness-1025336
3. Being able to film, edit, do sound, and/or special effects at one workstation.

References

Anand, N., Peiperl, M. A., & Arthur, M. B. (2002). Introducing career creativity. In M. A. Peiperl, M. B. Arthur, & N. Anand (Eds.), *Career creativity: Explorations in the remaking of work* (pp. 1–12). Oxford, UK: Oxford University Press.

Ball, S. J., Maguire, M., & Macrae, S. (2000). *Choice, pathways and transitions Post-16: New youth, new economics in the global city*. London, UK: Routledge Falmer.

Bourdieu, P. (1984). *Distinction: A social critique of the judgement of taste* (R. Nice, Trans.). London, UK: Routledge.

Ching, D., Santo, R., Hoadley, C., & Peppler, K. (2016). Not just a blip in someone's life: Integrating brokering practices into out-of-school programming as a means of supporting and expanding youth futures. *Horizon, 24*(3), 296–312.

Erstad, O., Gilje, O., Sefton-Green, J., & Arnseth, H. C. (2016). *Learning identities, education and community: Young lives in the cosmopolitan city.* Cambridge, UK: Cambridge University Press.

Facer, K. (2011). *Learning futures: Education, technology and social change.* London, UK: Routledge.

Gilje, O., & Groeng, L. (2015). The making of a filmmaker: Curating learning identities in early careers. *E-learning Digital Media, 12*(2), 212–225.

Gregg, M. (2011). *Work's intimacy.* Cambridge, UK: Polity Press.

Gunz, H., Mayrhofer, W., & Tolbert, P. S. (2011). *Introduction to special section: Careers in context* [Electronic version]. Retrieved from Cornell University, ILR School site: http://digitalcommons.ilr.cornell.edu/articles/50

Hodkinson, P. (2008). *Understanding career decision-making and progression: Careership revisited.* Proceedings from John Killeen Memorial Lecture, London, October 16, 2008. Retrieved from https://pdfs.semanticscholar.org/6d4a/5a943645032f4aa9336c41ece01b4598eb5e.pdf

Hodkinson, P., & Sparkes, A. C. (1997). Careership: A sociological theory of career decision making. *British Journal of Sociology of Education, 18*(1), 29–44.

Mathieu, C. (2012). Careers in creative industries: An analytic overview. In C. Mathieu (Ed.), *Careers in creative industries* (pp. 3–35). London, UK: Routledge.

Moore, C., Gunz, H., & Hall, D. (2007). Tracing the historical roots of career theory in management and organisation studies. In H. Gunz & M. A. Peiperl (Eds.), *The handbook of career theory* (pp. 13–38). Los Angeles, CA: Sage.

Oakley, K., & O'Brien, D. (2016). Learning to labour unequally: Understanding the relationship between cultural production, cultural consumption and inequality. *Social Identities, 22*(5), 471–486.

Peiperl, M. A., Arthur, M. B., & Anand, N. (2002). *Career creativity: Explorations in the remaking of work.* Oxford, UK: Oxford University Press.

Savage, M. (2015). *Social class in the 21st century.* London, UK: Pelican.

Sefton-Green, J., & Brown, L. (2014). Mapping learner progression into digital creativity: Catalysts & disconnects. *State of the Art Review* for the Nominet Trust. Retrieved from www.nominettrust.org.uk/sites/default/files/Mapping%20learner%20progression%20into%20digital%20creativity%20FINAL.pdf

6 Higher Education, Intellectual Property, and Incubation Mechanisms

The Case of Australia's Indie 100

Phil Graham

Pedagogies of Experience and Some Principles for Creative Incubation

Indie 100 began at Queensland University of Technology (QUT) in Brisbane, Australia, as a research project into the rapidly changing production and distribution environment that continues to affect revenues, laws, production practices, and the commercial wranglings of music business and music industry alike. In 2011, the project enlisted and engaged local, national, and international professional networks to produce 100 new songs over six days in May and promote them throughout the following year. It became quickly evident during the 2011 event that it held many benefits for the musicians who participated, for the students who worked in it, and for the profile of Brisbane independent music more broadly. The project was thereafter enlisted as a pedagogical device for university students of music, creative industries (CI), and entertainment industries at QUT annually until its final year in 2015.

The pedagogy of the event has been theorised elsewhere as an example of a 'Deweyan experience economy' (Graham, Dezuanni, Arthurs, & Hearn, 2015). The line of that argument runs as follows. The 'knowledge monopoly' of universities, held since Christmas day 800 AD and having survived every new medium up to the Internet, has been so thoroughly upended by platforms such as YouTube, Google, and the Internet Archive, that the higher education (HE) sector needs to entirely rethink its place in society. Given the informational flood associated with the new media, the sector-wide impulse to 'put everything online' using MOOCs and such is understandable but quite likely misguided, not only because students can be unfamiliar with or unaccepting of the means of communication used for online pedagogies (Cowie & Sakui, 2014) but also because there is simply so much rich information available on almost any topic imaginable through open platforms that any thought of maintaining HE's centuries-old knowledge monopoly by adding more information to the environment is simply nonsensical.

The experiential demands of CI education also fly in the face of informational pedagogies. Music is exemplary in that respect. No amount of instruction about, say, recording and mixing a piece of music or playing a musical instrument can ever possibly substitute for the experience of actually making music. The answer, then, at least as far as creative pedagogies went, was presented to us as a course of high-quality, high-stakes, highly visible curated experiences in which students directly connect as professional peers with other more experienced and better-connected professionals.

Incubation is an ambiguous term in the CI. The question was continually raised throughout the project, 'Do we aim our efforts towards artist, song, project, or scene?' The answer was inevitably a mix of all four, with shifting emphases depending on the stage of the project's annual cycle. In its initial stages of announcement and promotion, we naturally emphasised the project's benefits to artists to attract participants with good songs. During the event, the project's emphasis typically shifted to particular songs as 'products' of the event, the artists who created them as 'stars' of the event, and the overall Brisbane independent music scene as progenitor of the artists and the main focus of the project's processes. After the event, the project's focus shifted firmly towards specific artists, in some cases helping them 'scale up' their activities through the project staff's extensive professional networks.

The European Creative Industries Alliance (ECIA) summarises the best-practice aspects of incubation for CI across five dimensions: facilities and equipment, financing opportunities, partnerships and networks, business knowledge, and internal management of the incubator (ECIA, 2014). By those measures and definitions, Indie 100 operated as a CI incubator. It provided artists and students with ease of access to world-class equipment and promoted 'specialist skills training activities' in both music performance and production (ECIA, 2014, p. 5). We effectively, though somewhat indirectly, provided 'financing opportunities' to artists by giving them production, distribution, and intense promotion free of charge. Two of the ECIA's key criteria for success along that particular dimension are 'raising awareness before traditional lenders' and 'providing assistance on the development of a strategic approach to effective value chains' (ECIA, 2014, p. 5). Traditional 'lenders' for musicians are recording and publishing companies whose 'loans' take the form of advances: sums of money awarded under contract which artists had to recoup from royalties before receiving further revenue distributions. The project connected participating artists with high-level representatives of major recording and publishing businesses through their inclusion as industry panellists. It also generated, disseminated, and promoted findings that helped inform 'the development of a strategic approach to effective value chains' (ECIA, 2014, p. 5) for musicians in the new digital network environment faced by project participants and did so through trade publications rather than solely academic outlets (see, e.g., Graham, 2012, 2013a, 2013b, 2015).

In terms of 'partnerships and networking,' Indie 100 conducted best-practice CI incubation to the letter by providing the benefits of 'collaborative sessions between research centres, industry and entrepreneurs, and from the participation in different events aimed at fostering strong links and exploring new partnerships or product/services development' (ECIA, 2014, p. 5). The project proved to be an excellent catalyst for new creative partnerships, with multiple new, long-term professional relationships forged during each annual event. And while our dissemination of 'business knowledge' tended to be more abstract, critical, and theoretical than the detail required for specific 'business modelling' exercises, the programmatic nature of Indie 100 led to many participants reaching 'an international scale' (2014, p. 5).

The ECIA recommends as part of best practice that incubator management team should participate in 'international projects and networks related to Cultural and Digital Industries to gain a deeper understanding of the sector' and foster 'close relationships' (2014, p. 5). We were fortunate to have on the project's original management team Mike Howlett, whose professional history includes starting Strontium 90, a group who, minus Howlett, would later become the Police. Howlett was also a founding member of Gong, a Grammy-winning producer for a Flock of Seagulls, Martha and the Muffins, Orchestral Manoeuvres in the Dark, Thompson Twins, Tears for Fears, Gang of Four, and innumerable other iconic musical acts. Similarly, through Andy Arthurs—another founding member of the management team, protégé of George Martin, and denizen of the UK's record industries—the project was introduced to national and international relationships which project participants leveraged into various levels of success. Julian Knowles brought national and international relationships to the project, as did I. The project's regular production staff, Lachlan 'Magoo' Goold, an ARIA award-winning producer, and Yanto Browning both introduced to the project extensive local, national, and international relationships.

The project displayed all the features of best-practice incubation identified by the ECIA. But that was more accident than design. Indie 100 was never consciously a CI incubation exercise; it was a research and engagement project in which a unique pedagogy of experience presented itself as a fruitful way forward for teaching CI professionalism in HE. That said, the central question that shaped the project is a more abstract version of the same one that must be asked in any process of CI incubation: 'How can this artist, cultural industry, or business best build a sustainable livelihood?' (cf. CEA, 2018). Indie 100 sought to answer the sustainability question for a whole sector at once. One of the answers is that the 'portfolio career' described by Bartleet et al. (2012), which is focused specifically on classical musicians as individual agents who meet their 'artistic needs through freelance performing work, while simultaneously engaging in more financially stable part-time work in music education or arts management' (Bartleet et al., 2012, p. 35), is not particularly relevant to the contemporary independent popular musician. For them, the project showed us, a portfolio career means roughly what Veblen described as being characteristic of the handicraft era of industry (1914/2006, Ch. 6). For the musician as a handicraft worker, virtuosity of workmanship must constantly be tempered by an equal facility for the commercial viability of all their activities, along with assiduous concern for monitoring and control of the copyrights they produce. Quite often, artists often take on composition, recording, sound, lighting, and management of their activities up to the point at which royalties and fees provide a means of professionally involving more and more people. As became evident in a series of interviews closely related to Indie100, musicians in the era of major labels had to carry a massive burden of 'service industries' and 'middle men' that multiplied its weight with success, including booking agents, road crew, road managers, studio costs, mastering costs, record company costs, publishing company costs, management, lighting and audio equipment hire, transport, lawyers, venue hire, manufacturing costs, graphic artwork—the list is almost endless (Graham, 2019, Ch. 12).

Innovation Frameworks in Australian Higher Education (HE)

The relationship between innovation and intellectual property in Australia's HE system is weird and fraught. Our public HE institutions have lately taken to setting up third-party, arms-length (though wholly owned) corporate subsidiaries sometimes called 'innovation centres,' through which all commercially focused innovations generated within the university are expected to pass. Requirements for including projects typically include exclusive assignment of all intellectual property to the university's third-party entity. There are quite practical reasons why that is the case, but the requirement can also repel innovators from outside the university and even constrain innovation (cf. Peter, 2017).

There are a number of reasons for that, chief among which is the fact that university innovation hubs have a strong focus on the commercialisation of patents, and it could be said that the innovation arms of Australian universities are simply not set up to commercialise what are termed 'creative outputs.' There are a number of successful initiatives in the area, such as Queensland University of Technology (QUT)'s Creative Enterprise Australia (CEA), and they tend to be more focused on incubation, offering inexpensive rents to creative start-ups, fostering access to professional networks and mentorship, providing workshop-style advice on business planning, and so forth. Entities like CEA tend not to take an interest in the intellectual property (IP) of creative works, instead acting as place-based incubators in which the restrictions and benefits of place are both played out (see, e.g., CEA, 2018). In institutional terms, they are more hubs for engagement than dedicated exploiters of university-made IP.

The somewhat separate approach to incubation and innovation for the creative sector by Australian HE institutions evidences the thorny nature of creative IP more generally. It is nowhere more evidently so than in the area of music where difficulties stem from tensions among different national and international bodies of copyright law, entrenched practices in the CI, and the way universities have to navigate IP for academic publications. (It is probably worth a separate piece to discuss the relationships between our universities' reluctance to be involved with owning or commercialising creative IP, the long history of academic publication practices, and IP clauses in Australian university employment contracts that specify any IP produced by employees is automatically the property of the university.)[1]

Students are, of course, a different matter. In the Australian HE system, students own their own IP with the university having no claim over their work except in cases where they are funded to work on a defined aspect of a research project. Such students are almost exclusively postgraduate research students. All of this is a very circuitous way to frame a project in which music students, staff, industry professionals, and a very large number of local musicians all shared in the mass development of new musical IP, creating a complex tangle of rights and exposing many ambiguities and complexities created by the way music gets made (its industry aspects) and the ways music makes money (its business aspects). It is also by way of rationale for how the project was eventually constructed, almost in spite of university IP protocols and tendencies.

A Brief Description of the Event

The event was part of a broader research agenda into independent music trends and their sustainability with a particular focus on the impact of new media platforms for the production and distribution of recorded music by independent artists. It annually aimed to produce 100 new songs in 100 hours over 6 days in 3 recording studios with 72 acts. Each year, the event involved local and national industry figures, between 300 and 400 local musicians and around 70 students from music, management, marketing, law, and entertainment industries.

The event began with a call for participation through a state peak body for contemporary music called Q-Music. Entries were assessed by an external panel of industry professionals to produce a final list of 72 acts who would be involved in the recording event. Industry reference groups acted as a two-stage 'filter' for the project, choosing the 72 acts that would be involved in the event from the hundreds of application received each year, and, following the event, the panel curated the recordings to shortlist songs for an annual 'best of' compilation album, which included two full days of re-recording for each of the successful acts as an incentive (see Indie 100, 2018 for a streamable collection of all tracks produced during the project).

The experiential aspect of the event means, first, putting students into a professionally realistic context in close contact with practicing professionals in a way that provides for 'continuity' of experience, both pedagogically and professionally (Dewey, 1938, p. 43). Secondly, it means that students are embedded into local communities that can form the basis of future professional relationships. Third, it means putting students to work with local artists (many of whom were also coincidentally students) in highly visible publicity networks, thereby providing the kinds of high-stakes pressure in which strong creative and personal relationships are forged. It is the kind of pedagogical 'situation,' which in Dewey's terms is 'inseparable' from the concept of pedagogic 'interaction' (1938, p. 43). Dewey puts it as follows:

> An experience is always what it is because of a transaction taking place between an individual and what, at the time, constitutes his [*sic*] environment, whether the latter consists of persons with whom he is talking about some topic or event, the subject talked about being also part of the situation; or the toys he is playing with. . . . The environment, in other words, is whatever conditions interact with personal needs, desires, purposes, and capacities to create the experience which is had. . . . The two principles of continuity and interaction are not separate from each other. They intercept and unite. They are, so to speak, the longitudinal and lateral aspects of experience.
>
> (1938, p. 43)

This exposition thus makes clear how Dewey's (1938) pedagogical criteria of continuity and interaction are met by Indie 100 and also emphasises the role of the event in connecting students with their professional environment.

The effects of the project were excellent for many of the acts involved, for the students who worked the project, and for the visibility of Brisbane independent music more generally. It involved more than 2,000 musicians over its 5-year life, dozens of producers, and hundreds of student assistants. At December 2016, a year after it finished, the project recordings were still generating an average of 329,567 streams per quarter across all streaming platforms for a quarterly return of AUD$2,063 to the project. The project generated almost no physical sales but generated over four million streams during the life of the project for just under AUD$20,000 in revenue. The streams came from 70 countries, including Guatemala, Croatia, Iraq, Kazakhstan, Moldova, Serbia, Ukraine, and Venezuela, along with all major global music markets. Its social media sites received over five million impressions during the life of the project. The project gathered 892 survey responses from participating artists between

2011–2015. The survey told us that our 'typical' participant was male, aged between 18 and 34, had been playing music for five years or less, and had no formal music qualifications.[2]

Numerous artists who came through the project went on to attract national and international acclaim. Some went on from the project to be signed to major labels in Australia or internationally. Multiple artists from the project won state music awards, with two winning national independent music awards. There were many broader apparent effects of the project, including a heightened percentage of Brisbane artists featured in the Triple J Unearthed charts (an Australian national broadcaster's chart for a youth indie audience) across the life of the project; international attention for specific artists, including one that attracted more than 1.5 million streams of one song over three years; an annual increase in new recordings released by local artists; and a generally heightened awareness of local music and musicians from both industry and public audiences.

Contextualising Changing Realities for Music Professionals

There is no shortage of evidence to suggest that recorded popular music was the first global business to be radically disrupted by digital communication technologies. The Napster debacle was the first to come to a head in 1999, and it was clear that the major labels were once again preparing to fight a new technology of distribution with all the legal force they could muster, even if they had to criminalise their audiences to do it (Graham, 2019, Ch 1). Interestingly, the majors, save for some relatively minor issues around sampling technologies, had no issues with the digital revolution in production technologies that began in earnest from the late 1970s and began the proliferation of small-scale 'home recording' studios. Nor did they take issue with the earliest of digital distribution media, the compact disc (CD), an innovation which, according to former Sony COO Michael Smellie, turned the recorded music business from a global network of what he describes as 'cottage industries' to a massive system of global corporations (Graham, 2019, Ch. 2).

In the political economic terms of Veblen (1914/2006), by the late 1990s, music production (or music industry) had begun to resemble a 'handicraft' economy (p. 216). That is to say, small independent producers had begun to proliferate, and they were increasingly taking responsibility for both production and exploitation of their music; they were fast becoming businesses *and* industries. There were, of course, still many famous residential and large-format studios throughout the world at that time, and the major labels all were having record years thanks to CD distribution. But by then, the 'home studio' had already become prevalent enough for the music production establishment to decry their existence and bemoan the inevitable loss of quality, fidelity, musicality, and so on associated with 'home studios' (Leyshon, 2009; Goold & Graham, 2018). Such was the industrial landscape when the final wall for DIY (distribution) came down in about 1999. All of a sudden, not only was 'anybody' able to compose and record release-quality music, now 'anybody' could distribute it on a global basis. They could send a perfect copy of their music anywhere in the world at close to light speed. Napster invented a searchable streaming database for music distribution, and the rest is history.

By 2011, we knew several things. The first was that the old business model for recorded music that had dominated in a relatively stable manner from the 1970s through to the late 1990s was finished and would never return. There was already evidence of a predatory backlash to the forces of decentralisation in the business arm of music, with schools, parents, colleges, and individuals being prosecuted by the majors for copyright infringements for downloading music (see, e.g., Latonero, 2000). Spotify had penned its first deals with the majors, and Myspace had already disappeared as any kind of influential force. Artists had already begun loud criticism of streaming royalty rates, with Coldplay being among the first artists to refuse to allow their music to be streamed by Spotify (Graham, 2012). Everyone was looking for answers. From Brisbane to Nashville to Cannes, music exploitation had shifted from the 'next big thing' in terms of talent to how new talent could, would, and should make their way to a sustainable future given social media, drastically cheapened production processes, clogged creative arteries and airways, the new streaming economy, and the massive scramble to be noticed from amongst the unglamorous morass of everything and everyone clamouring for fame, fortune, and, most of all, attention.

The Indie 100 IP Complex

To understand the business of music in the new environment required the project (as 'the university') to take a controlling interest in the IP. We also needed to ensure that contributing artists could freely commercialise the tracks we recorded and retain ownership of their IP. The university consequently put itself in a position of being an erstwhile combination of record company, aggregator, and research enterprise. The artists signed an agreement upon applying for the project that gave the university a license to commercialise the material produced during the event, with proceeds to be split 50:50 with artists once the project had recouped costs against returns. It became clear very quickly that the project would never recoup at an aggregate level. The very conservative estimate of costs for the project ran at a nominal AUD$25,000 per year, which included a rough estimate of staff time, payments to professional producers, cost of video documentation, printing, advertising, and the many other incidental costs involved in running the project.

Artists had the right to commercialise the track separately to the university, with a reporting obligation to the university being triggered after more than $5,000 income was generated by the artists' commercialisation efforts. Artists were also given the right to purchase their raw sessions (individual tracks as recorded on the day) for $250.00 to remix or do whatever they wished with them, without further obligation to the university. Development of the artist contract naturally spilled over into research ethics and publicity requirements of the project. Artists committed to having their music, correspondences, videos, and images used as part of the research; to providing the university with a permanent, royalty-free license to use the material for teaching and research; and to participate in a survey (see the aforementioned).

Because Australia's 1968 Copyright Act specifies that all who take part in the recording of a musical work share in its ownership, the IP complex for the project was further complicated by the contributions of volunteer labour by postgraduate and undergraduate students. Other complications were generated by relationships among songwriting and performing personnel in bands, and by vague understandings about ownership and control of IP and its commercialisation. For example, there was not a year that went by in which one or more artists did not request removal of their material from one or more of the platforms on which it was distributed (usually Spotify). In some cases, we were easily able to oblige; in others, we were not. The most typical reasons for artists wanting material removed was to release a different recording of the same title or because the recording did not reflect the artist's changed aesthetic since the recording was made (all requests for takedowns except one in 2011 were made one or more years after the artist was involved in the project).

The scale of the project led to multiple complexities in IP exploitation. Simply releasing the material became a formidable challenge. In the first year of the project (2011), we planned with our distributor to release the first 100 songs on EPs of 4 or 5 songs each week for 20 weeks, following the event. The release plan included a physical CD release for each EP. Lead times were long as a consequence of the physical releases and the initial plan quickly fell apart and was prohibitively expensive. The aim of the EP release was related to a disproven hypothesis about audience attention spans. The release schedule was developed according to the hypothesis that releasing tunes in EP-sized 'chunks' serialised weekly over five months would extend interest in the event over time. That was not to be the case. First, the event was the time during which audience attention to the event peaked, rapidly dropping away afterwards. I offer a snapshot of the project's Bandcamp statistics by way of demonstration (see Figure 6.1):

Figure 6.1 Indie 100 Bandcamp Plays, 2012–2018

(Source: https://indie100.bandcamp.com/stats#zplays)

Each of the peaks is at the start of the annual recording event. We see here a phenomenon that project members came to understand as 'the novelty principle' (Brown, Graham, & Knowles, 2010, in Brown, 2010). The novelty principle states that a pronounced aspect of newness for new digital music

> feeds directly into its success. . . . Even at the very basic level of a fleeting appearance on a music community's front page for a single musical work, the novelty principle goes to work, lighting up the back catalogue and driving traffic to the artist's profile.
>
> (2010, p. 112)

The principle was evident in every release and in every Internet medium, including the project's Facebook page, Twitter account, YouTube channel, and all other web interfaces, for the entirety of the project and without exception. It was still evident with each staggered release, but the further we got from the date of creation, the less pronounced the 'peaking' effect of the novelty principle.

The initial release plan also failed in terms of timing. Rather than taking 20 weeks to achieve, we were still releasing material right up to the start of the 2012 event, a full year later. This had to do with production and distribution logistics. They included holdups with artwork, CD pressing, mastering processes, lost or missing files, and changes to project personnel. There were also major failures in metadata organisation—a function of the sheer chaos of the initial event—which held up communication with our distributor to generate International Standard Recording Code (ISRC) registrations for each track. Given the failure of our initial release plan, and a more refined understanding of the novelty principle, in 2012, we began the move towards rapid release of the entire project within the time frame of the event; our aim became to have all the songs recorded during the event mixed, mastered, and released to the project's Bandcamp site within the six-day envelope of the event. It took us four years and hundreds of practical mistakes to achieve that single aim. Worldwide distribution through our distributor, MGM, would necessarily take a little longer than the Bandcamp posting because of metadata requirements for ISRC registration of the year's output and the related labour at MGM in entering the data and uploading tracks to various platforms.

Changes in the release plans had a distinct effect on what was or was not practical in terms of actioning requests from artists to remove material from online commercial distribution platforms. The requests, though few in number, served a useful function in highlighting the complexities and practical implications of IP relationships for the project. Our contract with MGM, while being *prima facie* strict and comprehensive, was largely negotiable thanks to our close relationship with company personnel and most especially with its CEO, Sebastian Chase, who generously helped the project team design the event and refine its operations across the life of the project. The main complications involved Apple Music and the need to make any changes album-wide. That meant to remove any track, MGM staff had to remove the whole album of which it was a part. Then the remainder of the album had to be re-entered and uploaded to make the album, minus whichever song an artist wanted to take down, available to the world again. Consequently, takedowns were easier when we were releasing the EP-sized collections of four to five tracks. But once we started releasing the collection as a giant 'album' of 100 songs or so, takedowns involved 99 other songs, their ISRCs, and other metadata, and so things got more complex.

I explain the takedown matter—small as it was as an issue in the overall project—to emphasise how quickly and how far the rights complex of the project became elaborated and entangled in practical terms, simply in the very basic acts of recording and distributing the songs. The Indie 100 project rights complex (or complications if you prefer) developed as follows: the university took a controlling interest in IP created by members of the public so the project could research the flows of attention and money associated with the production of recorded music. We split rights to commercialisation in two, with both artist and university having a right to commercialise with multiple and mutual obligations involved for each party. While the university funded the recordings in large part, the recordings could not have been made without the work of the many dozens of volunteers who participated in the recordings each year, both as impromptu performers and, more routinely, as assistant engineers. As a matter of federal legislation, that makes the volunteers 'in principle' partners in the IP of any recording in which they participated on a voluntary basis. Then, to distribute the tracks, we assigned a comprehensive array of rights to our distributor so it could license the recordings to different streaming services, consequently invoking and entangling the project in a whole other web of global contracts, rights, and obligations. The same thing happens with any material that is posted online to any platform: it invokes and involves the terms and conditions of each platform, and is immediately involved in multiple rights regimes across the globe. There is undoubtedly a thesis in tracking down the implications of the many webs of legal to-ing and fro-ing involved in the emerging rights complex of recorded music because there are multiple public, private, national, and international laws bearing on the commercial life of any given recording on a streaming platform, many of which are worth billions in aggregate, most of which are still being worked out (Castillo, 2018).

In some circumstances, the effects of the distance between the two sets of rights (songwriting and recording) were evident at the coalface of the project. For example, between recording a particular song during the 2013 event (May), the selection of the song by the compilation panel (July), and the re-recording of the track for inclusion on the compilation (early August), there had been a personal falling out between two of the band's members. One had written the lyrics, the other the music. The song's composer left the band, and some kind of détente was required for the re-recording to happen with any degree of comfort for the remaining band members, especially for the lyricist. While there was no legal barrier to re-recording the track, the artists involved were keen to avoid any public 'political' fallout about the re-recording, and so project staff helped broker an informal agreement for a recording of the song to take place in which the composer refused to take part.

Again, all of this is to emphasise how far and how fast the rights complex spread beyond the project, the university, the artists, the distributor, and anyone else with a direct material interest in the music created during the project. The few participants who asked for removal of their music from Spotify and iTunes received insights into how quickly control is ceded once any kind of aggregation and distribution agreements are in place for recorded music, and how complex and frustrating disentanglement can be despite the best efforts and intentions. Even though the project's agreements were written with the artists' rights foremost in mind, and never to the commercial benefit of the university or the project, the project required a right to commercialise. That single requirement drew every participant in the project into a web of agreements that extended globally in vague, complex, and often unfair terms (Graham, 2015).

For independent artists, collecting revenues—something which ought to be easy compared with the requirement for call-centre quantities of clerical work in the major label era—is now more complicated than ever, thanks to an apparent increase in the number of people involved in the value chains of commercial music in the digital streaming era (Graham, 2012). In fact, entirely losing control of copyrights among the many shifting online platforms, agents, and agencies is easier than ever thanks to global reach and ease of replication and mere corporate repackaging, as with the sale of Aimee Street's catalogue to Amazon Music (Graham, 2012, 2016).

Portfolios: Social and Individual

And so to the 'portfolio' of skills demanded by contemporary independent music professionalism: to be successful in independent commercial music, now a sector with larger market share than any single major label (World Independent Network, 2017), some kind of musical virtuosity or uniqueness is but one of many 'entry requirements,' the far more pressing of which include an ability to 'get along' collaboratively, a flair for friendly publicity, an understanding of the commercial landscape and its changing means of sustainability, at least a basic mastery of audio and visual technologies, a keen understanding of copyrights and intellectual property, and an equally keen understanding of how to control them. An understanding of production processes and aesthetics is essential, as is the need to understand the range of agents and agencies involved in the business of music. Above all is the need for successful independent artists to develop and maintain a reputation for professional integrity, something that involves a commitment to music as a social service, something useful to others, whether professional peers or audience members, rather than as primarily an expression of one's artistic 'identity' or emotional state, or a faithful conservation of some mediaeval performance or another. None of these is a 'skill' that can be taught through the mere delivery of information. Each is a manifestation of experience, reflection, and relentless but gentle critique from peers. The idea that good music is all about the musician—*art pour l'art*—is possibly the most harmful of all ideas about what being a professional musician means, if only because it provides a basis on which to lower payments to musicians, rationalise pay-to-play engagements, increase competition in an already hypercompetitive field, and confound issues of business and industry (Graham, 2015).

The pedagogical potentials of Indie 100 to develop those qualities became evident very early in the relatively short life of the event. The project's characteristics included high-quality plant and equipment; high-stakes, high-visibility, high-intensity exposure to industry professionals, both within and beyond the bounds of the event itself; and an engaged approach that allowed students to build local relationships in what one participant describes as the 'speed dating of music recording' (Lang, 2015). For young musicians hoping to make a living doing something that takes more time to learn than being an airline pilot, yet is lucky to attract the most modest of payments, the event offered a sense of hope by demonstrating the power of collaboration. Wendy Lang describes the feeling of being involved as an artist:

> Musos get to feel like they're part of a special music community all striving towards a common goal. When Indie 100 is on, I feel like maybe—just maybe—the sum of all of us musicians meeting, collaborating and simultaneously recording, may inadvertently create a musical movement to be known in years to come as *Indiepressionism*.
>
> (Lang, 2015)

That the event consistently attracted the attention of local, state, and national media; the collective intensity of the experience Lang describes; and the many long-term relationships that formed amidst the manic pressures of the event all speak to the social character of music professionalism. To educate aspiring 'stars' into a collaborative and socially conscious mindset where music is concerned can be a challenge when the cultural myths and *mores* around notions of success in music (and other art forms) all point to the primacy of a few innately gifted individuals (Montuori & Purser, 1995). The effects of those myths can be seen throughout music, from the dogged yet questionable idea that one-to-one instrumental lessons should take a central place (or indeed have any place at all) in the higher education of musicians, to the many discourses about 'selling out' to market influences, to the studied 'ironic' contempt for all things commercial being regurgitated at virulent rates amongst certain subsectors of popular music.

Conclusions

Indie 100 began as a deliberately spectacular engagement- and research-driven 'stunt' to enlist the talents of new and emerging artists in Brisbane, Australia, primarily in order to understand how they could make a sustainable future for themselves in music and to bring the scene as a whole into national prominence. It was only to the extent that we were actually doing something, especially by way of providing deep connections with industry and business alike or by generating public profiles for artists through related performances and promotions that we were successful in our broader practical goal to help the local sector in any visible way. Once the project stopped, its effects fell away as quickly as those of any cultural novelty.

The project generated such pedagogically productive results by engaging students in professional networks beyond the university that we embedded those approaches in the pedagogy of our music degrees at both the undergraduate and postgraduate levels. We began, as it were, taking an incubation-style approach to teaching our students: providing them with excellent infrastructure, offering them access to local and global networks of expertise, incorporating expert knowledge of business and industry, and most of all, providing expert-led experience in understanding and negotiating the terrain of fast-changing distribution and exploitation landscapes. Even students who participated by managing the event have done remarkably well from the project. Sam Shakespeare, one of the project team in 2012, says,

> Just after graduating I moved to Sydney where I worked for The Premier Harbour Agency. Since then, my life has changed a lot. I now live and work in Vancouver, Canada, where I am a project management assistant at Macklam Feldman Management, one of the world's most successful music management companies. . . . Working on the 100 Songs project and starting a music blog, *Mind the Music*, really set me on my way.
> (Shakespeare, 2018, in QUT Creative Industries, 2018)

The stories of success and tragedy that came as a result of the project, among students, staff, and artists alike, would take a book-length project and some years to track down in any detail, such was the scale, complexity, and intensity of the project.

I have deliberately not emphasised the paradoxes of the project—for example, that our approach to understanding exploitation of rights involved us taking part in exploitation, regardless of how artist-centric we tried to make it. Such paradoxes are no doubt obvious, if not comically so, to the reader in their irony and, I should say, practically unavoidable given the aims of the project. Throughout, the prime culprit in terms of taking up labour time was the complex and relentless issue of copyrights and IP. The idea for the event, initially and flippantly floated by Andy Arthurs at the end of a meeting, came in 2010 following QUT's Big Jam event (QUT, 2009). It took a full two years to organise the first event, most of which was taken up with figuring out how to deal with copyrights and contracts.

Our development of what turned out to be best-practice incubation was a happy accident related to our 'Deweyan experience economy' approach. It provided an environment in which students, artists, and professionals alike could interact with genuinely professional levels of exposure, pressure, and intensity; have time and encouragement to reflect upon the project and their performance in it, both in terms of failure and success; and extend the life of the project through ongoing collaborations that continue into the present day.

The individualism of the 'star' system, in both music and academia, plagued the project at every level. It became for me the main 'enemy' in terms of what I saw holding back the success and sustainability of musicians and their musical careers. It is yet another paradox that we addressed the related hypercompetitiveness of music professionalism with something that resembled (from some perspectives) a music 'competition.' Despite its potentially competitive 'front,' the project engendered a positive communal thriving that was evident in statistics and qualitative comments of all kinds, and which undoubtedly came from a sense of friendly competition during the event. Who could record the largest group in the smallest space? Who could record the most songs in the four-hour time frame? Who pulled the best sounds during any given event? Who could do the most sessions in six days? Which tracks got played and featured beyond the project, whether by our national broadcaster, local radio, or press? In the heat of the project, those were the kinds of questions that were answered by word of mouth through the building. But the achievements of the project were collective, in which students, staff, and artists shared alike. They were self-consciously collective, with individualism getting short shrift in any particular session or on any particular issue. In investigating a scene, we helped build a scene. In building a scene, we learned and taught the value of sociality and sociability. We shared techniques and lessons with each other, multiplying the value of experience, whether that was the experience of years or the experience of youth. Both were invaluable to the project.

Notes

1. The challenge for IP ownership where academic publishing is concerned comes directly from the fact that academic publishers usually require assignment of copyright to the publisher. That is a grey area given that Australian universities, by default, own the copyright to each book, chapter, article, and conference paper written by any of its employees, thanks both to federal copyright legislation (Commonwealth of Australia, 1968) and common IP clauses in university employment contracts, which claim rights to any and all IP generated by employees. So if the academic publishing process were to be consistent with national copyright law, it would require the university to assign the rights for any given item to the publisher. In practice, though, universities leave that to individual academics for many reasons that are no doubt obvious, if only from the standpoint of bureaucratic cost alone. Hence the university tends not to claim publications as corporate copyright and that tendency extends to the creative arts in general, with the 'literary' status of scholarly publications seemingly at the base of the practice.
2. Seventy-four per cent of respondents were male, with most aged between 18–24 (434 respondents) and just over 85 per cent aged between 18–34 (697). Sixty-three per cent had been playing music for five years or less. Twenty-one per cent were degree-qualified, and 45 per cent had no formal music qualifications at all.

References

Bartleet, B., Bennett, D., Bridgestock, R., Draper, P., Harrison, S., & Schippers, H. (2012). Preparing for portfolio careers in Australian music: Setting a research agenda. *Australian Journal of Music Education*, 1, 32–41.

Brown, H. (2010). *It's not me, it's you: A participant observation case study of the self-publishing musician in the 21st century*. Brisbane, Australia: Queensland University of Technology. https://eprints.qut.edu.au/view/person/Brown,_Hugh.html

Castillo, M. (2018, February 28). Music streaming service Spotify files to go public, lost $1.5 billion last year. *CNBC Tech News*. Englewood Cliffs, NJ. Retrieved from www.cnbc.com/2018/02/28/spotify-files-for-ipo.html

CEA. (2018). *QUT Creative Enterprise Australia helps start, grow, scale and connect creative companies*. Brisbane, Australia: CEA. Retrieved from http://qutcea.com/

Commonwealth of Australia. (1968). *An Act relating to copyright and the protection of certain performances, and for other purposes*. Canberra: ACT. Retrieved from www7.austlii.edu.au/cgi-bin/viewdb/au/legis/cth/consol_act/ca1968133/

Cowie, N., & Sakui, K. (2014). Take your pick: Out-of-class, blended language and Web 2.0 Projects, and online. *JALT CALL Journal*, 10(3), 273–286.

Dewey, J. (1938). *Experience and education*. New York, NY. Touchstone.

ECIA. (2014). *Best incubation practices aimed at supporting creative & digital businesses*. Brussels: Cluster 2020.

Goold, L., & Graham, P. (2018). The uncertain future of the large-format recording studio. *Proceedings of the 2017 12th Art of Record Production Conference*, Royal College of Music (Stockholm)/Journal on the Art of Record Production.

Graham, P. (2012). Digital value chains for music promotion, licensing, and sales. *Music In Australia Knowledge Base*. Sydney, NSW: The Music Trust. Retrieved from http://musicinaustralia.org.au/index.php?title=Digital_Value_Chains_for_Music_Promotion,_Licensing,_and_Sales

Graham, P. (2013a). Australian copyright regimes and political economy of music. In P. Tschmuck, P. L. Pearce, & S. Campbell (Eds.), *Music business and the experience economy: The Australasian case* (pp. 11–26). Berlin: Springer.

Graham, P. (2013b). The cost of uncollective unconsciousness. *Music Forum: Journal of the Music Council of Australia*, 19(2), 14–17.

Graham, P. (2015). *Issues facing fair compensation for musicians in the era of streaming*. Sydney, NSW: Music Australia. Retrieved from http://musicaustralia.org.au/2015/06/issues-facing-fair-compensation-for-musicians-in-the-era-of-streaming/

Graham, P. (2016). Paradigmatic considerations for creative practice in creative industries research: The case of Australia's Indie 100. *Creative Industries Journal*, 9(1), 47–65.

Graham, P. (2019). *Music, management, marketing, and law: Interviews across the music business value chain*. Berlin: Springer.

Graham, P., Dezuanni, M., Arthurs, A., & Hearn, G. (2015). A Deweyan experience economy for higher education: The case of the Australian Indie 100 Music Event. *Cultural Politics*, 11(1), 111–124.

Indie 100. (2018). *Indie 100: Bandcamp*. Brisbane, Australia: Queensland University of Technology. Retrieved from https://indie100.bandcamp.com/

Lang, W. (2015). *Indie 100: Like the speed dating of music recording*. Retrieved from www.wendylang.com/home/2015/6/15/indie-100-like-the-speed-dating-of-music-recording

Latonero, M. (2000). *Survey of MP3 usage: Report on a university consumption community*. Los Angeles, CA. Annenberg School for Communication, University of Southern California. Retrieved from https://learcenter.org/images/event_uploads/mp3.pdf

Leyshon, A. (2009). The software slump? Digital music, the democratisation of technology, and the decline of the recording studio sector within the musical economy. *Environment and Planning, 41*(6), 1309–1331.

Montuori, A., & Purser, R. E. (1995). Deconstructing the lone genius myth: Toward a contextual view of creativity. *Journal of Humanistic Psychology, 35*(3), 69–112.

Peter, S. (2017, August 8). Do innovation centres undermine innovative thinking? *Australian Financial Review*. Retrieved from www.afr.com/brand/boss/do-innovation-centres-kill-innovation-20170714-gxbd3d

QUT (2009). *Q150 big jam live music event*. Brisbane, Australia: Queensland University of Technology. Retrieved from https://researchdatafinder.qut.edu.au/display/q56

QUT Creative Industries. (2018). *Creative Industries 2018 undergraduate courses*. Brisbane, Australia: Queensland University of Technology. Retrieved from www.qut.edu.au/__data/assets/pdf_file/0010/257752/creative-industries-ug-courses.pdf

Veblen, T. (1914/2006). *The instinct of workmanship and the state of the industrial arts*. New York, NY: Cosimo.

World Independent Network. (2017). *Wintel worldwide independent market report 2017*. Warwick, UK: Warwick University. Retrieved from http://winformusic.org/files/WINTEL%202017/WINTEL%202017.pdf

7 Guiding Young Creatives in the Last Mile

Ben Kirshner and Adam York

Although a central purpose of this book is to showcase young people's agency and ingenuity as they seek and sustain work in creative industries, these are not solo journeys. Our research is full of examples of key others—sometimes mentors, sometimes teachers, sometimes gatekeepers—who played critical roles coaching young artists and brokering their access to creative networks and industries.

Understanding the roles that key others play in guiding young people's artistic pathways is important for a few reasons. First, because creative fields tend to be less gated by certificates and formal school credentials, networks and relationships take on greater importance. This is especially the case for young people from marginalised groups or those without formal higher education degrees who may not have connections to paying industry positions (Ashton, 2015; Bridgstock & Cunningham, 2016). Second, prior work on mentoring and brokering has focused primarily on dyadic psychosocial mentoring or relationships between paid staff and youth within youth organisations. Few studies have examined what brokering looks like as youth navigate the 'last mile' into creative industries.

Our chapter draws on data sets from arts programmes for youth and young adults in two cities, London, UK, and Denver, Colorado, USA, to generate an initial typology of different kinds of guidance performed by more experienced others to support access and opportunity in the last mile—the final steps into work, see Chapter 1. These data allow us to combine young people's narratives about key guidance elicited in interviews (London) with observations of guidance based on field notes (Denver).

Understanding the Problem: Access to Work in the Creative Industries

There is mixed evidence within the literature about access to careers in new media arts for youth from marginalised or minoritised backgrounds. On one hand, as suggested by other chapters in this book, there has been some public and philanthropic support for community media organisations and youth programmes that support access to and skilled production of new media and digital arts. In the US, these include initiatives such as the Digital Youth Network (Gomez, Barron, & Pinkard, 2014), Youth Radio (Soep & Chávez, 2010), and Hive NYC (Ching et al., 2016. Efforts such as these aim to ameliorate the opportunity gap facing youth from marginalised backgrounds by offering guidance from skilled profession-als, access to quality technology, and opportunities for agency and digi-tal production (e.g. Barron, Gomez, Martin, & Pinkard, 2014; Soep & Chávez, 2010). There is also evidence of efforts by older youth—in their late teens and early 20s—to self-organise networks and communities that nurture digital media production (see Chapters 1 and 2).

At the same time, research has shown that employment in the cre-ative sector is still very much gated by factors such as higher education degrees, social networks, and family wealth, which in turn are closely correlated with race and class (Ashton, 2015; Guile, 2009; Oakley & O'Brien, 2016). A recent study by Oakley and O'Brien (2016) reports that '78% of the UK media industries workforce hold an undergraduate degree (p. 476),' suggesting that, despite its open qualities, creative indus-tries still privilege qualities associated with college going. They argue that it is not necessarily the content of the degrees that matter, but instead the practices of self-cultivation common to the middle and upper middle classes, 'beginning with the bewildering variety of extra school activities undertaken by some middle class children in childhood,' which confers 'competitive advantage for the labor market' (p. 478).

The less credential-driven quality of the creative industries places a pre-mium on relationships, networking, and social capital (Ching et al., 2016; Lee, 2011). Filmmaking and public art have rich histories, and there are many experts in the field who have insider knowledge and can assist young people in finding a path within these domains. However, structured or intentional guidance is scarce outside of the university and for-profit art schools, which require aspiring creatives to take a financial risk. Addition-ally, because of historical underrepresentation of women and people of colour in these fields, many artists from marginalised backgrounds find it difficult to find and form connections with mentors or brokers who can understand their backgrounds and help them with challenges related to dis-criminatory practices and glass ceilings. Moreover, as discussed in Chapter 8, the greater opacity of how one arrives at a career in new media arts elevates the importance of more experienced others who can make the domain vis-ible and broker access to opportunity. Such assistance goes beyond interper-sonal mentoring to a hybrid combination of personal support, coaching in navigational skills, and brokering new relationships and opportunities. For the sake of parsimony, we call this range of activities 'guidance.'

But what does this guidance look like?

Guidance in New Media Arts

Studies of youth media production spaces have made progress identifying the kinds of support and assistance that more experienced others provide

(Ito et al., 2013; Chávez & Soep, 2005). These are learning environments that emphasise creativity and the pursuit of interests, high levels of peer support and collaboration, and opportunities to produce and showcase work for valued audiences (Scott & Vella, 2015). Studies emphasise a form of guidance rooted in traditions of apprenticeship learning, which involve novices learning alongside skilled practitioners in a context of care and support (Rogoff, 2003). Richards and Gomez (2010), for example, highlight a practice in the Digital Youth Network, based in Chicago, to hire skilled artists in particular fields to act as mentors and teachers. Spoken word poets and hip-hop artists, for example, offer workshops for aspiring artists where they model expert practice and develop relationships with learners. From this process, young people learn not just the skills associated with the field, but they also begin to see what it looks like to develop a career; the path to becoming a poet or hip-hop artist becomes more visible.

A second more recent theme in this work is the emphasis on 'brokering' (Barron, Martin, Takeuchi, & Fithian, 2009; Cartun, Kirshner, Price, & York, 2014; Ching et al., 2016). Beyond supporting identification with the artistic field or skill development, brokering refers to ways that key others can connect young people to specific opportunities or networks. Barron et al. (2009), for example, documented varied kinds of brokering by parents, including creating access to opportunities, signing children up for programmes, and exchanging information with other parents. Ching et al. (2016), in work with programme practitioners, define brokering as 'a practice that depends upon and serves to strengthen relationships between youth and resourced individuals' (p. 6) and that is characterised by verbs such as 'bridging, connecting, guiding, linking, networking.' Ching and colleagues suggest that brokered connections are mediated by youths' help-seeking orientation, trust between the youth and the broker, and the broker's knowledge of opportunities for the youth to continue interest-related pursuits. We build on these lines of work by focusing more squarely on this issue of the 'last mile' (see Chapter 1), specifically looking at the types of guidance that facilitate access to paid work and artistic development.

Guidance may also take place in less instrumental ways than brokering. In fluid and emergent fields, such as spoken word or street art, there may not be stable institutions or well-known figures (O'Connor & Allen, 2010). In this context, guidance might look less like introducing or connecting people to insiders, but instead building new institutions and opportunities, as will be discussed in Chapter 8. It might also mean helping to make visible networks and activities that are otherwise opaque.

Our goal in this chapter is to develop a typology that documents different practices that facilitate access to creative industries in the last mile, drawing on a data set that prioritises young people's own perspectives and experiences. We intend this typology to be generative without claiming it to be comprehensive.

Data Sources

We draw on two different sources of data to begin to identify specific brokering practices. The first set comes from Julian Sefton-Green's set of interviews with black filmmakers in their 20s and early 30s in and around London, England (see Chapter 4). Analysing these data was critical because it permitted us to understand, from the perspective of young creatives, the kinds of assistance and brokering that were most helpful to their own professional opportunities. It enabled us to move beyond the intentional youth programme and examine brokering in the context of people's struggles to launch and sustain careers. We asked, 'What practices did interviewees share in their stories that were helpful to their access to employment or professional development in the creative domain?'

In analysing these interview transcripts with young filmmakers, we recognised that there might be some types of practices that are more observable by an ethnographer that would be less likely to be made explicit in an interview. In other words, there might be practices that facilitate access that are not likely to be narrated by a young person but could be discerned through careful ethnography. To address this, we drew on an ethnographic study completed by Adam York (co-author of this chapter) of a youth arts program, Riverplace Arts, which introduced high school–aged youth to 'creative civic practice.' During the time of his fieldwork, this programme hired a young adult professional artist to lead young people in the creation of a mural. In the process of documenting the learning in this setting, Adam observed how this artist offered guidance about what it looks like to find and sustain a livelihood doing public art with a focus on addressing injustice. We draw on this data set to answer, 'What practices did we observe in field notes that appeared important for supporting young people's pathways to work in creative arts?'

To generate our typology, we first worked separately to identify and name all excerpts of data from the interview data set relevant to the first question. After analysing these interviews and identifying relevant excerpts, we discussed our results with each other to identify areas of convergence and divergence in our choices, and to generate an initial typology. We then went back to Adam's observational notes to see if there were themes in his data that either converged with our typology or suggested new categories. This hermeneutic process of developing categories in one data set, checking them against another data set, and then exchanging ideas with each other was followed through several iterations. During this time, we further refined the phenomenon—guidance in the last mile by more experienced people—in order to finalise the typology for this chapter. We acknowledge that this is meant as a suggestive typology rather than a conclusive one, primarily because of the unique qualities of the two data sets. An appropriate next step would be to test these categories against the experiences of other young creatives and what they describe about key forms of guidance en route to creative work. To present our claims, we begin by sharing two case examples, and then we transition into the different kinds of guidance.

Navigating the Last Mile: Case Examples

Idris

Idris was a freelancer seeking and sometimes finding employment in the filmmaking industry in London, including as production assistant, camera operator, and director. His stories about seeking to find opportunity and secure work reveal some of the themes related to guidance that showed up in our broader sample.

Idris described frustration and challenge in figuring out how to land paid work in filmmaking. He didn't find formal education in film to be of much use—his teachers did not show passion or interest in him as a person. Moreover, there were few black instructors or programme staff, and he did not feel that the people there understood where he was coming from. He tried to take advantage of access to equipment and his relationships with people in the rap and music video scene, and was able to land some work doing music videos. He was resourceful, seeking out new contacts and leveraging existing relationships to gain new ones.

For Idris, project work helped form the right kind of connections. It was a friend-of-a-friend connection, beyond his programme ties, that allowed him to advance his career. He remembers,

> At the time, like I was always involved in a . . . project, because I would talk to everyone about video and stuff. And there was a guy who I met, and he . . . had shot music videos which had been on TV, and that . . . for me, was the next step up.

This contact took a while to turn into work. As Idris said, 'He didn't take me seriously . . . until I started working with M. [another person respected in the scene].'

Although Idris's resourcefulness and knowledge of the music scene helped him begin to find work, Idris grew frustrated with his progress and sought out a different kind of guidance—less about instrumental contacts and more about mentoring in how to navigate the field in general. Idris asked for advice from a person who worked at a local arts training organisation he attended (called WAC). He said, 'It literally just felt like, damn, I feel like I needed someone, I needed a mentor, something. And I went to Catherine [who worked at WAC].' Idris recalled a conversation he had with Catherine as they discussed opportunities through applications or new connections he was seeking: 'I said, "I need someone that's going to help guide me, because I don't know exactly what I'm doing."'

For Idris, support from Catherine, as well as other programme staff at WAC, was pivotal to gaining new contacts and receiving care and support as he navigated the industry. As he gained new opportunities, he continued to learn and observe from those who had found success. He recalled an opportunity on a set where the assistant director (AD) was black, and he thought to himself, 'Wow, there's a black person on set and he's an AD, and how the hell did you do it, sort of thing?' He described how this person, Sekani, 'helped me out a lot.'

Later in his interview, Idris told a story of an industry connection made by a friend, which resulted in a paid deal. The friend helped Idris get into an industry function, and while the monetary incentive was for his friend, there was still personal meaning in that connection for Idris. Idris recounts,

> One person for him at the time sort of was a great contact because he helped him get his foot into Universal and then we got him a deal. And, for me, just seeing all of that again just sort of built. . . . It ignited my passion.

Idris's stories illustrate how much intention and effort it took from him to seek out mentoring and contacts to help him with his career. Although the help was offered by key others—sometimes inside the industry, sometimes not—we can see that he learned how to actively recruit that help and then drew lessons about how people did things once he gained opportunities. Idris acknowledged this tension too—as he both sought out help but also saw the task of figuring out his 'destiny' as his own. Idris did the personal work of developing his craft while aware of the value of meeting the right mentor.

Manny

Idris's example illustrates an aspiring filmmaker's experiences of guidance and how important it was to form connections to industry insiders. The example of Manny, taken from a public arts programme where youth interns worked on a mural project, differs from the earlier case in two important ways. First, this case describes guidance *offered* by an experienced professional rather than reflections by youth about guidance *received*. Second, this example blends guidance regarding the practical elements of finding paid work with guidance regarding finding one's creative path regardless of employment or income.

Manny was a hip-hop artist and eco-activist who was a guest speaker at Riverplace Arts. The stories he told the young aspiring artists revealed lessons about the role of other mentors and social networks for artists seeking to sustain careers in public art. While some forms of guidance, such as brokering new contacts and relationships, leads directly to industry connections, other forms of guidance have more to do with helping aspiring artists understand the field and how they fit in it. This latter emphasis, conveyed primarily through storytelling about his own life and the role of art in it, was the focus of Manny's guest appearance.

Manny's narrative opened with a statement of his own artistic identity and how he got there.

> Yeah, you know. I'm a hip hop artist, and it's just important. . . . I didn't always know I was an artist until I became a part of what we call a hip hop movement, and now I could be hip to all kind of different artists and, like Jeff was saying, you don't have to be classically trained to be an artist, you just got to tell yourself you're an artist and then start doing it, so that's what happens.

Manny's guidance was grounded in personal experience where the title of 'artist' is inclusive of people from many backgrounds and is earned more by engaging in a set of practices than formal training. Success for him was something beyond income or recognition, and had to do with life-changing practices and connections.

He continued,

> Your life could take new roads, you could meet new people and you pave the way for yourself to be an artist. That's mad important. When me and Jeff met, when we met we weren't even good buddies at first, but through art we squashed the silly beef and we like tight as hell, yeah. . . . It does good things for your life.

For Manny, success in art was primarily about the human connections one can form, with the possibility of paid work as an ancillary benefit. While the connections that Manny discussed were primarily peer-to-peer among practicing artists, the message that connections starting with mutual interests can 'pave the way' to something greater asserts that social connection is an important factor in finding success and resonates with the other practical examples we encountered of brokering leading to greater opportunities in the field.

Manny discussed the social component of artistic work and mentioned how art can transform relationships between people. Manny was invited to speak to these interns by Jeff, a prominent local graffiti artist who was leading the interns in the production of a public mural. Though Jeff and Manny engaged in different art forms, their work intersected, and through their work, they grew a personal connection based on an interest in the power of creativity for social change.

Manny reflected on the value of creativity, beyond instrumental goals for income or career. He wanted the students to think of their work in relation to a community history and a broader public good.

> These projects that we're talking about: can we sustain, or how in the future . . . can (we) sustain the world for the better of it? Creating the

art that can sustain the history and the knowledge of these few past months to the next generation . . . if we can extend that, it's going to keep coming up, this is an important factor of being a public artist.

Manny underscored the connection with friends and colleagues as a natural outgrowth of the creative work that served to strengthen bonds between people and support their artistic dreams. He concluded with a vision of the importance of public art that highlighted the intergenerational connectivity that holds meaning beyond paid work, specifically to include serving future generations through creative work.

Summary of Cases

We selected these two cases because they showcase some of the varieties of guidance valued by and offered to young artists as they learned about and pursued careers in the field. Idris, in discussing his creative biography as a filmmaker, recounted how he cultivated mentors and industry connections in order to find paid work on projects and learn the ins and outs of mature industry practice. His stories showcase the interdependence between his agency and hustle and his efforts to recruit mentoring by industry insiders. Manny's homiletic narratives, on the other hand, offered as educational messages to young artists, reveal a different type of guidance—more focused on making the domain of public art visible and its connections to valued relationships and community connections. The two examples show similarities in reference to the importance of connection, but important differences in the way artistic work figures into a person's life. In Idris's case, he was following industry connections to sustainable work. Manny's artistic work supported stronger relationships and greater opportunities rooted in a particular vision of public-oriented art outside of market incentives.

These are just two examples intended to bring to life the range of what guidance can look like. We now turn to a more systematic typology based on the types of guidance we observed in our data.

A Typology of Guidance Practices in the Last Mile

We distinguish between general types of guidance and creative industries types of guidance, the latter of which were specific to finding work or developing careers in film or related artistic endeavours (see Table 7.1).

Table 7.1 Types of Guidance

General	Creative Industries
Assertive encouragement	Technical content and skills
Coaching in generic professionalism	Validation of talent
	Brokering key relationships and networks
	Making the domain visible

General Types of Guidance

Assertive Encouragement

Respondents described key moments when other people encouraged them or pushed them to carry out their education or work goals. Multiple filmmakers recalled programme staff at WAC or family members telling them they needed to sign up for a particular opportunity. Nathan described getting 'a really good push from my mum.' Toma spoke about the pivotal role played by the founder and director of WAC:

INT: Okay. So she said, so she basically said, you should be going to film school.
TOMA: Yes. She said you need to go to film school.
INT: Right in no uncertain terms.
TOMA: And you need to apply now.
INT: Okay, and you thought okay.
TOMA: I was at a point where I knew I needed to do something, I didn't know what, I trusted her, so I thought, you know, okay, let's try it.

Others also spoke of key interactions where they were told to take advantage of or apply for an opportunity. Josh, for example, recounted an adult who he knew saying to him, 'Why don't you apply for the National Youth Theatre? I think you'll really love it.' So he applied. Another respondent, Linda, talked about a key teacher who got her excited by telling her to 'just go for it.'

In the case of Riverplace Arts, advice for interns was formally built into the programme through dedicated time for personal work with mentors and a culture where encouragement and opportunity sharing were common features of day-to-day conversation. Staff members encouraged interns to enter their creative work into local art shows and explore educational and career opportunities, such as scholarships for postsecondary education.

Coaching on Generic Professionalism

A closely related form of guidance was to lend advice about *how to* apply for things or follow-up on a professional contact. Here too respondents talked about receiving guidance from valued teachers or family members, not just industry professionals. This was recalled by filmmakers who asked for help with curriculum vitaes or resumes from more experienced individuals. Valerie told a story about an arc of learning that began with her mother showing her how to follow up on a key contact, which she eventually learned to do on her own:

So my mum . . . she was like, 'Have (you) emailed that guy?' And I was like, 'No I don't know what to say.' So then she would help me form an email. And then give it another month and she would say, 'Have you emailed that guy?' 'No, I don't know what to say.' 'Just form another email,' she would say. So . . . (later), whenever I did my own stuff like Sickle Cell . . . this time no one needed to tell me, I just told him, and he was like, 'Oh Valerie, come down; we're doing like a work placement ad for a company.'

Valerie went on to describe how she showed up at the interview and earned a paid work placement at the film company, which was key to the launch of her career.

Coaching in professionalism and how to seek opportunities was also present in the structure of the Riverplace program. High school–aged interns were required to complete regular professional development workshops, such as how to apply and interview for jobs. Program staff encouraged interns to use them as references when seeking career opportunities.

Guidance in the Creative Industries

The aforementioned examples of assertive encouragement and coaching in finding employment, though important, did not require that the guidance be provided by an established artist or industry insider. The remaining practices that we identified in our data, however, presupposed interaction with a more experienced artist or insider. The role of the more experienced industry figure was illustrated in the cases of Idris and Manny, with Idris seeking specific insider connections to get further and Manny leveraging his credibility as a socially conscious hip-hop artist to lend advice to youth. Other interviews and observations repeated this core theme that aspiring artists sought mentors and brokers who had technical competence and, more important, industry experience. Those who had had succeeded in their industry or field had greater credibility, in contrast to teachers in institutional programmes or training centres. Idris spoke to this kind of credibility when he described his effort to reach out to a person with music video experience:

IDRIS: And there was a guy who I met, and he was, he had shot like music videos which had been on TV, and that was, for me, was the next step up. I wanted to . . .
INT: Where did you meet this guy?
IDRIS: I met him through a friend of a friend of a mutual friend, basically. So he . . .
INT: Nothing to do with WAC (arts and film training program)?
IDRIS: Nothing to do with WAC at all. . . . But I had met him, and I heard that he did videos which had been on TV.

Another respondent, Linda, talked about how much she valued her connections to a filmmaker, 'because . . . he's able to be quite successful in how he gets his films screened. . . . They're screened internationally and nationally and in nice cinema spaces.' Valerie appreciated people with experience who could provide a wealth of knowledge of the field. She listed some of the credentials of a person who was a key connection for her:

> He, like he has a sense of history, he's worked for the BBC; he's created . . . one of the departments in the BBC . . . he went over and worked with Discovery in America; he now goes to oversee production companies, for CTTV, so he's got like a wealth of experience.

Respondents contrasted industry professionals with teachers or instructors in film schools or programmes, dubbed by Linda as 'stuffy old men kind of teaching the same thing to every class.' Toma, for example, highlighted elements of his film school experience that were missing:

> Okay the massive problem with film school is, there's two things that they should have taught us, but they never did. They should have taught us how to actually access a career in film rather than just teaching us a load of skills then dumping us. And they should have taught us how to do our taxes as a freelance filmmaker . . . those are two things they did never teach us that seriously, it was just ridiculous.

Jermaine spoke to questionable expertise and knowledge among teachers, who 'seemed to never really be on top of what it was they were meant to be teaching us.' The priority placed on up-to-date skills, quality equipment, and practical experience represented threshold qualifications for mentors in the last mile.

An additional theme related to qualifications for trustworthy guides, which was raised by some, but not all, respondents, was the value of mentors with whom they shared similar life experiences and racial backgrounds. Several of the filmmakers highlighted the value of brokering by or relationships with more experienced people of colour. This was part of what Valerie mentioned about her expanding networks:

> There's this one guy who's now, who works at the BFI . . . and he's of the older generation. . . . He said he's missed opportunities because of his color and things like that. And now he wants to do this kind of thing where he can network with like young, not young people, just any professionals in the industry can like network together.

As Idris also noted, this is important because of the limited opportunities for young professionals of colour to find mentors of colour. As mentioned in his case summary, for Idris, encountering a project where there was a black AD on set was a rarity; he attributed his current success to the help and guidance of that person. Other filmmakers spoke to the importance of solidarity around shared marginalised identities for making connections and gaining access to opportunity. Valerie, for example, recounted pivotal support from other women:

> I think her name was T. . . . and then Women in Films is an organization that just helps women get into films, and she contacted me saying, 'I know you want to produce something, I've got work, can I introduce you to the director, can you like talk?'

In the Riverplace internship program, both Jeff, the lead artist, and Manny, the guest speaker, identified as artists of colour—as did a majority of the interns. We think this shared quality contributed to an interactional space where discussions of race and socioeconomic status were routine and ongoing. Such conversations informed the design of the mural and enabled young people to connect their social identities to discussions about artistic opportunities and aspirations.

Technical Content and Skills

Although one could make the case that teaching apprentices technical skills is separate, conceptually, from guidance in the last mile, because it is more about a skill than about fostering access, we include it here because of how integrated technical guidance was in people's accounts of what mattered to them.

The filmmakers spoke about the importance of specific guidance in skill development from people who they respected in the field. For example, one of the filmmakers, describing a program, said, 'They helped me there because they actually told me how to edit; otherwise, I would have never learned how to actually press the buttons and put it together in the first place.' These opportunities included multiple aspects of making films. Another interviewee learned from an instructor how to craft effective stories and their centrality for creating a good documentary.

This type of technical assistance was woven throughout youths' experience at Riverplace. Interns received direct technical instruction in drawing and graffiti from an accomplished professional, Jeff, who had created public artworks throughout the area. Drawing, which became a routine part of their meetings began when Jeff asked the group, 'How many of you can draw? How many of you like to draw?' Nearly all of the interns raised their hands, and Jeff continued, 'All right. Then all these ideas? You guys should be drawing.' They used the time in these meetings to sketch ideas for the mural. Jeff supported this and encouraged the group to draw whatever came to mind by relating examples from his experience. He walked the interns through the technical process of going from sketches to a large-format mural.

Because Jeff's focus was public, socially engaged art, some of these technical skills unique to the domain involved connecting with local communities. He showed the students how to create pop-up scenes on street corners and under bridges where student artists could hold extended focus groups or impromptu conversations about people's perspectives on the art and the history of the community. Here, the backgrounds of the artist and interns, as people of colour from the neighbourhood and surrounding neighbourhoods, became especially important in conversations taking place on the street in front of the mural. Interns discussed the impact of industrial expansion and pollution on low-income communities and how race factored into the history and future of the community. Jeff offered guidance in community-engaged art that attended to the dynamics of race, class, and history by encouraging public dialogue on those topics.

Validation of Talent

Validation from industry insiders played a pivotal role for respondents in the filmmaker sample. This showed both in terms of affirmative examples of validation and the devastating consequences of not feeling validated. Here, for example, Nathan described feeling like a 'piece of shit':

NATHAN: Art school was an absolute nightmare because my teacher made it her systematic duty to make me feel like I was . . .
INT: Useless.
NATHAN: A piece of shit basically. And I'm not sure. I think she had it out for me. I'm pretty sure she did because she'd tell me I'd fail. Like, every single time I went into the lesson, she always dragged me out and shouted at me and that, kind of, really aided my hate for secondary school at that stage.

On the flip side, Valerie talked about how valuable it was to have a teacher who showed interest in her work and sponsored her art through promoting it on public platforms.

I had another teacher . . . who I still talk to today, he's just like, he loved everything I was doing, it was like 'Valerie can I have more?' And he kept showing, like every time I did anything, I would tell him, 'oh I did this,' and the next thing I know it's on the university website. He's like linking it to everyone else, like, 'Okay, thanks.'

Here the teacher did not just provide validation in the sense of praise, but actively supported Valerie's work by posting it on the website and broadening her audience.

Brokering Key Relationships and Networks

We identified multiple examples in our data where experienced artists or teachers introduced young filmmakers to specific people or professional networks. Filmmakers spoke of how important such introductions could be for their ability to navigate and secure new opportunities. Idris, for example, described how he sought out specific opportunities to grow his skill set.

> For me, at the time, it was, 'I need to build contacts.' On the film set of *Breaking and Entering*, I had befriended the line producer. I told her that I really want to work in film, and she was really friendly . . . she got me in with the editor on another film that she was working on, so that was good. And they were so helpful, because anyone they knew who may have benefited me in any way, they sort of passed on the contact.

Similarly, Valerie described a connection that started with the WAC programme and then enabled her to get involved in other networks and activities.

> There's one of the . . . activities they assigned, that was with this guy S. (a graduate from a national film and television school), and he's tried to start this network up. And so I'm talking to him and he's linking, he's constantly, keeps bringing me in because sometimes, I'm always at home and I don't really always go out that much. So he's like this person, he'll meet up with people and network, which I'm trying to do more of now.

Staff in the WAC programme encouraged the practice of forming personal connections across the field. For Valerie, this led to greater opportunities to work alongside seasoned professionals in the industry. She described the way she took this connection and grew it into opportunities for other youth artists.

> He's creating, he's making a feature film, and it's all about gentrification and you know it's a statement, in the time of Columbus. So I'm creating a project alongside that where we have young people who are going to be working alongside these feature films, working with these people who are actually in the industry and making the films.

Making the Domain Visible

The aforementioned examples are rooted in interpersonal connections and relationships—they are about facilitating precious access to skills and people. The practice of making the domain visible, on the other hand, is about clarifying the contours of a field and what it looks like to make a life in it. This theme was less evident in the filmmaker interviews and more evident in our observations of the public art youth programme in Colorado. This may be in part because of the different types of data in the two locations: interviews privilege people's own insights and accounts of what mattered, whereas observational data put a spotlight on the verbal guidance offered by experienced artists in moment-to-moment interaction. A second reason for this theme showing up more in Colorado may be because of the type of art: public murals. Unlike film, which is relatively familiar and visible in popular culture, public art, particularly the kind of mural art that was the focus in Colorado, may have been less familiar to the youth interns, thus prompting Jeff to allocate more time describing it to learners. Also, because the youth interns were still in school and not actively seeking jobs in the creative industries, the programme leader focused more on introducing and making visible core aspects of life and work in the field. (The importance of making the field visible is further described in Chapter 8, which contrasts the relative opacity of creative industries next to established pathways, such as STEM careers). In this chapter, we have identified a few specific ways that veterans lent assistance by making the domain visible.

Jeff, for example, showed commissioned pieces he had done that covered the sides of multi-story buildings, murals alongside major roads, and privately commissioned pieces on the sides of businesses. He told the interns about his own studio nearby where he had recruited friends and other working artists to convert an old storage warehouse into a collective where they kept their work and stored tools, serving a spectrum of creative pursuits including sculpture, aerial dance, and a small T-shirt business (which he also noted was how he began to establish financial independence).

Jeff also worked to make the domain visible through telling histories of public art. These public works ranged across different topics and social issues that were of concern to the artists who created them and the viewers and residents of the places where the works reside. One day, Jeff carried in a crate full of books containing prints of the work of his favourite artists. He set this crate down on the table and began tossing books across the table, one to each person in the group. He shared that these examples demonstrated what he considered to be some of the best of murals and public artwork that had taken place both in the city and around the world. These works included many different Chicano artists who took up issues of immigration, farming, labour rights, and public and media perceptions of particular communities.

Jeff's efforts to make the domain visible for young artists also included insider accounts of how to work with other artists, clarify roles on teams, and get commissions for projects. In describing how he approached work similar to what they would be working on together that summer, Jeff foregrounded the importance of collaboration:

> I can't just take on a project like this by myself, and there's certain things that I could do, but there's people that do them much better. That's their thing. To be able to put people in position like that, once you have a team like that, you can do huge projects.

Lest it appear that this practice of making the domain visible was only observed in Colorado and not mentioned by the filmmakers in London, we did see some examples of filmmakers talking about the value of experiences that showed them a more holistic picture of the industry. Lilian, for example, gave a specific account of how work with a mentor led to a greater awareness of the possibilities within the domain of filmmaking:

> P. kind of really opened our eyes into the world that exists out there . . . people that are making work that we're making. He took us over to a film festival in France called FID Marseilles, and there's all this amazing stuff over there, which is exactly the sort of genre that we would probably fit into. So it was quite eye opening to see that it's possible to do that as well.

Conclusion

This chapter examined forms of guidance in the last mile. Whereas there is a large literature about the role of adults as teachers in youth development programmes, and a still vaster literature about how mentoring can be a vehicle for youth development and resilience, there is far less research about the kinds of mentoring, brokering, and coaching that young people recruit in their efforts to find and sustain artistic work in the new creative economy.

We found that this form of guidance sometimes grew out of relations of care, such as with parents or educators who pushed young people to pursue new opportunities and coached them in general self-advocacy strategies. There were also key forms of guidance in the last mile that were embedded in shorter-duration relationships linked to jobs, gigs, or social interactions. For example, consistent with the emergent literature on brokering, one of the most powerful forms of guidance, as reported by the young filmmakers, was being connected, introduced, or given access to industry professionals. This brokering of opportunities was most useful for those seeking paid work in a precarious freelance economy. It could be performed by friends, fleeting contacts, teachers, or employers.

But brokering was not the only kind of assistance we observed in these data. We also saw a key role played by those insiders who could validate the talent or vision of emerging artists. This validation, most useful when coming from industry insiders, offered confirmation or reinforcement of young artists' identities and commitment. Also important, particularly in less familiar domains or those where credentials are less salient, such as the ecosystem of socially engaged public artists in Colorado, was the practice of showing and describing the field for young aspiring artists. In other words, sometimes there is not an obvious 'insider' to whom to broker an introduction, or the field is not so settled or stable. Some fields may be off the beaten track enough that young people are not aware that they exist, or they don't have mental models of what it would mean to pursue them. In these contexts, more experienced artists offer guidance by showing the way: both by modelling an identity for youth and breaking down the various relationships and ideologies that stitch together these diffuse or hidden networks.

In these senses, the kinds of guidance we observed included, but were not limited to, instrumental economic relationships. Yes, particularly for those filmmakers in London hustling to support themselves in the creative economy, financial incentives were important, and connections to paying work were valued. But guidance was not merely an economic transaction. Several of these same London filmmakers expressed appreciation for mentors and guides who expressed a racial consciousness or political consciousness in their work and built networks to support that. Similarly for the public artists in Colorado, becoming a public artist required an entrepreneurialism (e.g. T-shirt selling) that functioned like a 'day job' but which was in the service of building community and honouring people and places through art.

Given the very place-based and field-specific nature of the two sources of data for this chapter, a key next step for this research is to test these categories against the experiences of other young creatives and what they describe about key forms of guidance as they pursue creative work. We view this typology as suggestive and likely to be further developed with research in other locales and attending to other genres.

One question that this analysis raises for us pertains to guidance as an intentional practice. Would it be feasible or useful for public sector or non-profit agencies to incentivise or structure any of the kinds of guidance described earlier? Although some, such as assertive encouragement and validation, can be reasonably expected to occur in the kinds of programmes described in this book, others, such as brokering, are most advantageous when there are willing and open industry people who see it as part of their work. What might it look like for that work to be incentivised or facilitated? There is a way in which the brokering experiences recounted by the London filmmakers had an accidental or idiosyncratic quality. How might industry brokering be less idiosyncratic and arbitrary, and more intentional about opening up access, particularly for young people on the outside of elite networks?

A second implication pertains to arts-based youth programmes. Our data support an argument that such programmes should broaden their horizons from an exclusive focus on young people's experiences within the time span of specific programmes to an emphasis on supporting youth after they graduate from programmes and navigate networks and industry relationships, especially those that link youth to artists with shared identities and backgrounds. Some cities, such as Denver from the case example, are connecting young artists of colour with mentors of colour through micro-grants. Riverplace Arts, for example, was funded through a city arts granting program. Another strategy would be to directly support networks of mentors whose purpose is to guide and broker opportunities in the creative industries for aspiring artists of colour or artists from marginalised communities.

References

Ashton, D. (2015). *Creative labour in the bedroom and on the web*. Paper presented at the conference 'Challenging media landscapes: Cultures and industries of creativity in contemporary media landscapes,' Manchester, UK, November 16, 2015.

Barron, B., Gomez, K., Martin, C. K., & Pinkard, N. (2014). *The digital youth network: Cultivating digital media citizenship in urban communities*. Cambridge, MA: MIT Press.

Barron, B., Martin, C. K., Takeuchi, L., & Fithian, R. (2009). Parents as learning partners in the development of technological fluency. *International Journal of Learning and Media, 1*(2), 55–77.

Bridgstock, R., & Cunningham, S. (2016). Creative labour and graduate outcomes: Implications for higher education and cultural policy. *International Journal of Cultural Policy, 22*(1), 10–26.

Cartun, A., Kirshner, B., Price, E., & York, A. (2014). Friendship, participation, and site design in interest-driven learning among early adolescents. In J. Polman, E. Kyza, D. K. O'Neill, I. Tabak, W. R. Penuel, A. S. Jurow, K. O'Connor, T. Lee, & L. D'Amico (Eds.), *Learning and becoming in practice: The International Conference of the Learning Sciences (ICLS) 2014, Volume 3* (pp. 348–353). Boulder, CO: International Society of the Learning Sciences.

Chávez, V., & Soep, E. (2005). Youth radio and the pedagogy of collegiality. *Harvard Educational Review, 75*(4), 409–434

Ching, D., Santo, R., Hoadley, C., & Peppler, K., (2016). Not just a blip in someone's life: Integrating brokering practices into out-of-school programming as a means of supporting and expanding youth futures. *On the Horizon, 24*(3), 296–312.

Gomez, K., Barron, B., & Pinkard, N. (2014). Introduction: The digital media landscape. In Barron, B., Gomez, K., Martin, C. K., & Pinkard, N. (Eds.), *The digital youth network: Cultivating digital media citizenship in urban communities* (pp. 1–13). Cambridge, MA: MIT Press.

Guile, D. (2009). Conceptualizing the transition from education to work as vocational practice: Lessons from the UK's creative and cultural sector. *British Educational Research Journal, 35*(5), 761–779.

Ito, M., Gutiérrez, K., Livingstone, S., Penuel, B., Rhodes, J., Salen, K. . . . Watkins, S. C. (2013). *Connected learning: An agenda for research and design.*

Retrieved from https://dmlhub.net/publications/connected-learning-agenda-for-research-and-design/

Lee, D. (2011). Networks, cultural capital and creative labour in the British independent television industry. *Media, Culture & Society, 33*(4), 549–565.

Oakley, K., & O'Brien, D. (2016). Learning to labour unequally: Understanding the relationship between cultural production, cultural consumption and inequality. *Social Identities, 22*(5), 471–486.

O'Connor, K., & Allen, A.-R. (2010). Learning as the organizing of social futures. *NSSE Yearbook, 109*(1), 160–175.

Richards, K. A., & Gomez, K. (2010). Participant understandings of the affordances of remix world. *International Journal of Learning and Media, 2*(2–3), 101–121.

Rogoff, B. (2003). *The cultural nature of human development.* Oxford, UK: Oxford University Press.

Scott, N., & Vella, R. (2015). Making music beyond their time: Training musicians for a future workforce [online]. In J. Rosevear & S. Harding (Eds.), *Music: Educating for life. ASME XXth National Conference Proceedings* (pp. 93–98). Parkville, Vic: Australian Society for Music Education.

Soep, E., & Chávez, V. (2010). *Drop that knowledge: Youth radio stories.* Oakland, CA: University of California Press.

8 Building and Brokering Pathways in New Media Arts

A New Dimension of Youth Programme Quality

*Ben Kirshner, Josephina Chang-Order,
Michael Harris, and Katie Van Horne*

The Growth of New Media Arts as a Focus of Out-of-School Time

Early research about out-of-school-time (OST) programmes tended to focus on programmes dedicated to mentoring, academic support, or youth leadership (National Research Council, 2002). Since the early 2000s, however, there has been steady growth in OST programmes that emphasise new media arts, including music recording, video production, photography, and web design, among other related media practices (Gomez, Barron, & Pinkard, 2014; Herr-Stephenson, Rhoten, Perkel, & Sims, 2011; Van Steenis & Kirshner, in press). These are settings where young people learn how to use digital tools to express themselves artistically, develop entrepreneurial skills, or broadcast social and political messages (Soep & Chávez, 2010; York, 2015). Unlike drop-in recreation centres, or even youth leadership programmes emphasising service or social action, these programmes offer opportunities for tangible skill development in the creative industries. Their growing popularity is noteworthy because one of the struggles facing OST programmes in the past has been the steady decline in numbers of teen participants as they depart elementary school and move into middle and high school (Deschenes, Little, Grossman, & Arbreton, 2010). New media arts programmes, perhaps because of their opportunities to learn new technologies, their focus on voice and expression, and the potential instrumental connections to future career interests, offer more compelling activities for older youth, particularly in low-income communities where young people may not have access to state-of-the-art digital tools (Gomez et al., 2014).

Following the New London Group's (1996) call for an expanded view of literacy—from text-based reading and writing to 'multiliteracies,' including video, music, and civic literacies—much of the research in OST digital media arts programmes has examined the kinds of literacies young people develop and how those relate to youth agency, ingenuity, and identity (Hull & Katz, 2006; Gutiérrez et al., 2017. Soep and Chávez (2010), for example, coined the term 'convergent literacy' to refer to a practice that young radio hosts developed when bringing varied types of stories and information to bear on one compelling radio story.

A second focus of the research has been on the social organisation of learning in these spaces (Barron, Wise, & Martin, 2012; York, 2015). Learning theorists have tended to agree on certain core practices that contribute to deep learning for participants, which reflect what scholars describe as 'connected learning' (Ito et al., 2013). These are learning environments that emphasise creativity, interest-driven learning, high levels of peer support and collaboration, and opportunities to produce and showcase work for valued audiences. In some cases, these audiences might be virtual, watching a video online, and in other cases, they might be face-to-face, such as watching a spoken word performance.

This research about the social organisation of learning finds that guidance typically resembles apprenticeship learning, which involves novices learning alongside skilled practitioners in an artistic domain. This means that in many new media arts programmes, the 'teachers' are practicing hip-hop artists, videographers, or photographers (Richards, Gomez, & Gray, 2014). Young people learn from these people not only technical skills but also what it means to be a professional artist or creative person in their respective fields.

In the research about youth digital media arts programmes, however, what has received far less attention is the role that programmes can play in supporting young people aiming to secure work or opportunities beyond the programme itself (see Chapter 1). This issue of transitions is especially salient in the digital media domain because, as a field, digital media is less dependent on school credentials and more reliant on networks (see Chapters, 2, 3 and 6). This calls for a shift in how programme staff envision their relationship to youth learners—from a focus on their experience within the time and space of the structured programme to a more extended relationship that supports post- programme transitions. Research about how young people construct pathways in digital media fields is especially needed because emerging research suggests that the new media arts domain has a high level of openness and precarity that is distinct from other occupations, particularly those that are gated by credentials or higher education degrees. In this sense, this line of research represents a contribution to the field of learning sciences, which has typically focused on learning in more institutionally stable and taken-for-granted domains, such as math or science (Penuel & O'Connor, 2010).

Theoretical Lens: The Social Organisation of Developmental Pathways

Our perspective, which draws on social practice theory and sociocultural learning theory, attempts to re-centre the focus of youth development research from either the young person or the bounded programme and instead towards the institutional fields that shape and certify what counts as mature participation (Bourdieu, 1998; Lave, 1996).[1] Take, for example, a youth programme focused on hip-hop music production. Conventional positive youth development (PYD) research offers well-developed frameworks for either individual outcome variables (e.g. improved music skills or more general social and emotional development) or programme features (e.g. quality of instruction or youth-adult relationships). But a focus on youth outcomes or programme quality distracts us from grappling in more complex ways with broader institutional and social fields that organise young people's pathways (Zeller-Berkman, 2010). This matters because understanding the fields to which young people aspire—what expertise or mature practice looks like, how it is—recognised and gains exchange value, and how access is controlled—has important implications for youth programme pedagogy. It might call for changes, for example, in the guidance roles played by programme staff or how organisations design and hold themselves accountable for youth outcomes.

In using the term *fields*, we draw on Bourdieu (Bourdieu, 1998; Warde, 2004) but also recent theorising in the learning sciences about *infrastructure* and *consequential learning* (Gutiérrez, 2008; Hall & Jurow, 2015; Jurow, Horn, & Philip, 2018). Here infrastructure includes material objects, but it also extends to social relationships, systems for recognising status, and values. Jurow et al. (2018) summarise infrastructure as 'the ubiquitous and often transparent networks of relations that allow for information flow, access to resources, and the maintenance of the social order' (p. 1). Closely related is the notion of consequential learning, which stresses that learning becomes *consequential* when it is recognised as valuable or aligned with institutional pathways in a field. To return to the hip-hop example, consequential learning in a hip-hop youth programme would be signalled not just by the qualities of youths' rhymes or technical skills, but in their alignment with the practices of hip-hop collectives, relationships with members of those collectives, and how their performances are valued and circulated among hip-hop listeners.

Consistent with the broader goals of this book, in this chapter, we offer a conceptual framework that clarifies pathways into mature practice beyond the boundaries of the youth program. This framework aims to denaturalise the routes that people take from novice to mature participation by surfacing the various kinds of active organising work that are required to build visible and socially supported pathways (Barron, 2004, 2006; Barron et al., 2014; Gutiérrez, Morales, & Martinez, 2009; Varenne & McDermott, 1999; O'Connor & Allen, 2010). As discussed next, in emergent or less stable fields, it is easier to see this organising work in action, in contrast to stabilised fields that are supported by recognisable credentials and institutional gatekeepers. To represent the variability of fields from relatively stable to fluid or emergent, we identify two dimensions: visible versus opaque and gated versus open.

Visible Versus Opaque

Some fields have more visible pathways into them than others. We characterise visibility by examining how clear and evident the benchmarks are to progress in the domain and whether examples are available that enable youth to imagine possible futures in the domains. For example, science pathways are marked by institutionalised activities, such as required high school courses, which can lead to higher education majors in science or engineering (O'Connor & Allen, 2010). These are fields whose 'logic of practice' has developed over the years, aligned with the sequential ordering of school subjects and years so as to become evident to those in dominant positions within society, even if they are still exclusive or hard to reach (Bourdieu, 1998; Lingard & Christie, 2003). Research in the learning sciences has traditionally focused on institutionally supported pathways such as these (Brown et al., 1989; Sawyer, 2005). In the new creative economy, however, youth pursue emergent interest-related pathways that are less visible and rarely facilitated by alignment across institutions.

For youth to imagine a possible future, it helps to be able to see how to get from their current situation to the desired end point or destination that is relevant to their skills and interests. Sefton-Green and Brown (2014) found that youth who were successful pursuing their interests into the workforce 'were able to relate their own learning or expertise to the wider employment market or forge links with outside communities' (p. 13). Having this visible link allowed youth to identify opportunities to pursue their interests within a domain or find people and places that could act as brokers to these opportunities (Ching, Santo, Hoadley, & Peppler, 2015). Newly forming fields, however, may be more opaque; pathways are difficult to locate, and youth are uncertain about where to pursue their interests, even if they have a vision of a future career. This calls for programme leaders or experienced practitioners to engage in active organising work. O'Connor and Allen (2010), for example, described how leaders in a slam poetry programme dedicated their time to organising events and creating networks to recognise youth's achievements as slam poets, because these forms of institutional recognition did not already exist.

Gated Versus Open

Institutional recognition, in the form of diplomas or certificates, is a common indicator that a field is relatively stable. Credentialing by institutions tracks movement along a pathway and can function to sort participants as more or less deserving of opportunity (Varenne & McDermott, 1999). Certain fields, such as medicine or research science, are so credentialed as to be 'gated,' in the sense that one can only be recognised as a mature or professional practitioner in that domain by following a specific sequence of degrees and tests. But many fields, particularly in new creative industries, are relatively 'open' in the sense that there are many paths to achieving recognition as a legitimate practitioner, and traditional academic credentials are less valuable (Lee, 2011). Seeing entrepreneurial opportunities within a field of interest can be a marker of openness (Neff, Wissinger, & Zukin, 2005). Finding work in open fields tends to be more informal and based on networks and relationships. Open is not synonymous with easily accessible, however, because the pathways may be opaque and paid opportunities scarce.

In summary, this framework offers a way to understand and differentiate available pathways into desired futures. We compare the perceived pathways articulated by youth involved in a STEM (science, technology, engineering, and math) programme with those in a new media arts programme and explore implications for youth programme pedagogy.

Methodology

Background About the Pathways Project

The Pathways Project used a collaborative research design that included the research team at the University of Colorado and youth ethnographers from four youth programmes that identified with the principles of Connected Learning.[2] These sites were geographically dispersed throughout the US. This study aimed to engage youth, most of whom were youth from underserved communities, in the planning, data collection, data analysis, and reporting of findings. For the purposes of this chapter, we focus on data collected from young people from two of the four programs: Young Creatives and STEM Mentorship.

Young Creatives

Young Creatives is a pseudonym for a non-profit youth organisation based in a city in the north-eastern US dedicated to community revitalisation through the arts. Young Creatives runs youth development programming for children, youth, and young adults in areas including community gardening, house restoration, fashion and design, photography, hip-hop dance and recording, photography, and literacy. Several of the programmes hire professional artists or digital media producers to train and mentor youth, such as in video production. Young Creatives also offers a competitive artist-in-residence programme for artists to live in a house refurbished by young people and in return, provide workshops and training.

STEM Mentorship

The STEM Mentoring program was based in a science museum in a different city in the Northeast US. The programme enables youth to work with mentor scientists affiliated with the museum. Students participate in an authentic research project over the course of the school year, starting with a summer institute. Students receive a stipend for their work throughout the year. In addition, students become eligible for college scholarships through their affiliation with the program, and the programme offers college entrance test preparation courses and college visits. For the school year, students work in groups of two or three with a mentor scientist in either life sciences or physical sciences. Youth must apply to be considered for a position within the program. To be eligible, youth must take at least three science courses offered at the museum. The STEM mentoring programme targets science-oriented youth with post-secondary aspirations in the 10th and 11th grades.

Data Collection and Analysis

The primary data sources for this chapter were transcribed interviews carried out by youth co-researchers from the two sites. Youth interviewed three different categories of people involved: peers who concurrently attended the program, alumni who had graduated, and mentors or staff who were currently employed in some fashion by the program. Peers were asked about whether they could see themselves continuing with their current skills or interests into the future; alumni were asked about what they had gone on to do after graduating from programmes at the site; mentors were asked about the pathways they envisioned for, or had seen their participants take, after developing skills at the site. In total, the team completed 24 peer interviews, 10 alumni interviews, and 12 mentor interviews.

Youth teams completed data analysis and identified findings that they presented to staff at their respective programmes and university researchers. A subset of youth researchers also co-designed and co-led a workshop at a conference for educators and researchers. Later, the authors of this chapter continued to analyse data from the project in order to understand young people's journeys into work (see Chapters 1 and 7). As we compared the interview responses across program sites, we began to notice different types of barriers and successes. Our process of memo-ing and collaborative analysis led us to identify key factors at play in youths' pathways to work: individual experiences within the site, the structure of the programmes, the field and its visibility and organisation, and the characteristics of the site. In the analysis that follows, we describe what interviews with youth and programme staff revealed about the broader social organisation of learning ecologies in Young Creatives and STEM Mentoring.

Evidence of Programme Quality

Data from Young Creatives and STEM Mentoring suggest that both programmes embodied features of high-quality programming identified in the literature (National Research Council, 2002; McLaughlin, 2000; Strobel, Kirshner, McLaughlin, & O'Donoghue, 2008). This similarity puts into relief the differences we observed across the two sites in young people's accounts about pursuing desired futures in creative industries or science. Three features of programme quality showed up consistently in interviews: sense of community, supportive relationships, and opportunities for skill building.

Sense of Community

Sense of community is built on the experience of physical and psychological safety and opportunities to belong (National Research Council, 2002). Youth at Young Creatives, for example, described the site as an alternative to some dangers faced on the streets of their city:

> Because it's fun, a great way to stay with your friends, it keeps you out of trouble. Most people that I know that don't go to Young Creatives, they're in trouble, just going downtown.
>
> (Peer interview, Young Creatives)

A mentor described Young Creatives as a place of shared purpose that was woven into the fabric of the neighbourhood: 'It was a community that I felt close to. It just seemed like such a warm, welcoming place where I could grow and I could help other kids grow' (Mentor interview, Young Creatives).

Supportive Relationships

Supportive relationships offer emotional support and scaffolding for learning or skill development. At Young Creatives, one of the peer interviewees contrasted their experience to typical experiences in school: 'First day, I met a wonderful teacher. . . . In school, I felt closed. Here there was one-on-one. There was communication. There was assistance and learning but in a fun way.' Respondents also conceived of support in terms of the connections the youth used to access pathways to internships and experience in their field of interest. During interviews, young people expressed gratitude for specific adults at the organisation and influential adults in their personal lives. An intern from STEM Mentoring, for example, described how an adult at the site was instrumental in helping her gain information about an opportunity:

> I got started here by hearing about it from someone at the museum who I met through university. He told me about the program and I investigated further and learned more about it and completed the courses and ended up in it.
>
> (Peer interview, STEM Mentoring)

At Young Creatives, a peer interviewee stated, '(The) first day I met a wonderful teacher. I met Miss B. It was a very amazing community and a positive place.'

Opportunities for Skill Building

Whether skills were for personal enrichment or future employment opportunities, sites provided both structured educational opportunities and linkages to outside programmes of interest. Young people at STEM Mentoring expressed appreciation for learning how to do authentic scientific inquiry and develop skills that were less available in their schools:

INTERVIEWER: Tell me about a skill or interest that you enjoy doing at [STEM Mentoring].
YOUTH RESPONDENT: I really enjoy the fact that I have some sort of academic freedom. And the fact that even with this freedom, I have some guide to understand exactly what I'm doing. As well as the fact that, even though I'm doing lab work, I know exactly what the end goal is and what we're trying to find. And that, sometimes, is lost in a classroom setting (peer interview, STEM Mentoring).

There was also no shortage of comments about skill development at Young Creatives in new media arts, such as photography and music production.

INTERVIEWER: One more question: Do you find Young Creatives as a way out for kids, as a way to help them succeed and find jobs and be better people?
MENTOR RESPONDENT: Absolutely. Just the skills you're learning, whether or not you take them. You may not be a fashion designer, but having those skills and being able to create something and take on a new role for yourself and like, 'Wow, I didn't know I could do that. What else can I do that I didn't know I could do?' That's what's really important. I think that's what's really helping these kids to be like, 'I can accomplish that. I can accomplish anything. I made an animation today. I'm going to go to the moon tomorrow.' Things like that, I think, it just gives them this idea that they really can just do whatever they want (mentor interview, Young Creatives).

In summary, the interview data suggested that Young Creatives and STEM Mentoring met threshold elements of quality PYD settings, including sense of community, supportive relationships, and opportunities for skill development. Where we saw respondent narratives depart from each other was in their accounts of pathways into their respective fields.

Differences in Pathways Across Sites

Cross-case analysis shows divergence in the visibility of pathways and openness of fields (see Figure 8.1). Whereas stories about STEM pursuits reflected gated, brokered, and institutionally supported pathways, stories about pathways into new media arts reflected greater openness and opacity. We share examples of distinct strategies developed by both programmes to support young people in their pursuit of Young Creatives and STEM Mentoring futures given these features of the ecosystem.

STEM Pathways: Visible, but Gated

Interviews and commentary from STEM Mentoring youth researchers suggested a STEM pathway that was visible and understandable to teens, but also highly selective and hard to access. By pathway, we are referring to young people's sense of where to find work in the field and what further steps were needed in order to proceed further into the career.

Across the interview data from STEM Mentoring, all four peers answered affirmatively the question, 'Do you know of places where you can find work that builds on skills and interests you learned at your site?' Moreover, they gave specific examples of the locations: universities, a community lab, hospitals, and a robotics company. Two of the four peers also indicated that they had applied for research opportunities at some of those locations.

Interviewees also articulated a clear sense of their futures in the STEM domain. Although they did not all have a specific occupation (or science major) in mind, for them, the pathway was visible. It included getting research experience, majoring in science at college, and then pursuing

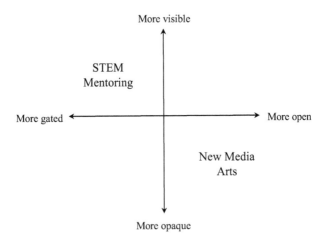

Figure 8.1 Differences in Pathways

further research opportunity. Ingrid, a youth participant, envisioned her career in the following way:

> I feel that I need to go through college in order to truly understand where I want to go [. . .] I'm planning to meet all the requirements that are needed for undergraduates and to go to a proper school to find the career that I want to go into and what science research I'm planning to do. Then, go to a graduate school and to . . . continue in my career path.
>
> (Peer interview, STEM Mentoring)

For Ingrid, the pathway was clear: obtain the requirements for applying to college, attend a school that would support her in determining what career to pursue, and then continue with graduate school in order to achieve her career goals. Although she didn't know for certain what she wanted to study or become in the future, later in the interview, she discussed specific career possibilities, such as basic scientific research or more applied research in the medical or bioengineering fields.

These narratives were accompanied by statements attesting to the challenges of accessing this pathway. Young people at STEM Mentoring talked about how it was difficult to find opportunities to engage in scientific research in their city because of a small number of highly selective opportunities, especially for youth. Beth, who stated a long-standing love for science and planned to pursue science degrees, was asked if she knew of places in the city where she could get a job that built on her interest in science.

BETH: Any university. There's the 'ARISE' programme at [university]. There is the science career ladder programme at the [name of museum]. There is the thing at [name of second university], where they have to take classes for three years and then do research there.
INT: Was it the neuroscience?
BETH: I think so, but there's another program. You have to take a placement test to get in.
INT: I feel like I know what you're talking about.
BETH: There is the thing at [name of program], with this young scientist thing. It's really hard to get into. There is [name of other program] with DNA bar coding. There is Genspace, which is a community lab.
INT: You know a lot.
BETH: I know a lot. It's hard to get into them. And it was really hard to get into this too (peer interview).

Beth's responses show both her awareness of opportunities and the ways in which they are restricted: one requires three years of classes, another is 'hard to get into,' and 'it was really hard' to get into STEM Mentoring.

Another student, Priya, told a similar story: scarcity of opportunity accompanied by awareness of where those scarce opportunities were:

> I really wanted to do science research for a while. STEM Mentoring was one of the ways that someone under the age of 16 could do research in [city].
>
> (Peer interview)

When asked how she found out about other opportunities to build on her experience at the museum, she talked about the variety of places that she could apply and all the people she had contacted. She explained how she knew about all of these opportunities by saying,

> (It took) insane amounts of internet trawling. You really have to search into these people and email them and see if any of them respond. Usually it's just 1 in 100 people who respond to emails sent out. So, it's a struggle.

An interview with a graduate of the programme showed a similar awareness of scarcity in telling the story of her interview for one of the internships. She remembered,

> I was like, semi crying. I was like freaking out because I'm never going to get this. Like six hundred people apply from all over the world. I was like, 'Well, I'm not getting it whatsoever.'
>
> (Alumni interview)

Young Creatives: Open, but Opaque

Young Creatives participants generated narratives about pathways that departed from themes articulated by youth at STEM Mentoring. We heard lots of success stories and gained a sense of a field that is open to those with talent, drive, and confidence. But interviews also suggested a more opaque and uncertain field with a less evident pathways; interviewees' statements about places to pursue interests or careers in the arts were not as precise or confident as those offered by the STEM students.

Kim, an alumnus of Young Creatives, offered a perspective that reflected the more optimistic, dynamic view of the creative industries. She described a wide range of possibilities for students interested in traditional and new media arts. In response to the question of where students could find work related to their interests, she said,

> Anywhere. Studios for dancing. School programs for mentoring. . . . So, you can actually start your own little daycare or summer camp or anything. You can go out in your backroom and have your little

fashion drawing and everything. Or, you can just go to school and further . . . education for your skills to get better, and then you can go into digital stuff for the art. You can go into vocal. . . . Sing at your school, sing at your church, just like better your music or your vocals until you think, 'Ok, I think I can do it.' You never know, they're people out there that haven't even had a job, sang in their backyard or their basement and everything, wrote their own music. Now, they're out there getting discovered from Atlanta or LA just by travelling and somebody hearing them sing. . . . You just have to put your foot forward. Don't be afraid to step out of that shower and sing in front of everybody else. So, you can find jobs anywhere. You just have to have an open mind and eyes and look for it.

This excerpt highlights Kim's perception of the openness of the new media arts field. Kim's examples were not related to gaining credentials or pursuing institutionalised pathways. Kim spoke to the availability of jobs through one's own initiative and creativity.

This quotation was emblematic of narratives from Young Creatives that, although sometimes mentioning the value of two- or four-year colleges, placed less emphasis on formal credentialing to access work in the arts. Interviewees at Young Creatives seldom mentioned the types of selectivity and scarcity barriers voiced by STEM Mentoring youth. Kathy, for example, who is interested in digital photography, described the openness of the new media arts ecosystem; she found photography jobs while also enrolled in Young Creatives programmes.

I've had [photography] jobs outside Young Creatives. . . . I've had jobs for the main library. Personal jobs. I've done baby showers. I've done stuff for my family. I do stuff for Young Creatives too, like when at the showcase I'm always the one who takes the pictures and stuff. I did graduations. I've done a lot of stuff.

(Peer interview, Young Creatives)

Kathy indicated later in her interview that she planned to attend college and start up her photography career afterwards, though she did not describe an explicit connection between the college degree and her photography plans.

At the same time as Young Creatives peers and alumni communicated a sense of openness and possibility, overall, their narratives show greater opacity and uncertainty relative to the STEM narratives. Consider these responses to the question, 'Do you know of any places where you can find work that builds on skills and interests you learned at Young Creatives?'

Example 1 (peer)
Lynn: No, I haven't heard anything like that. Not yet, but I'll look into it.

Example 2 (peer)
Paula: Not really.

Example 3 (alumnus)
Gene: I personally do not know, but if anything, I can recommend Young Creatives as a good place to start. They can help you find anything you like.

Example 4 (peer)
Kathy: I've had jobs through Young Creatives. It all started here. It's just Young Creatives for me.

Tonya, whose comments were an exception to this pattern, responded by saying, 'The only places I really know of that would catch me on something like that would be the City Theater Company and Sigma Sound.' Tonya wanted to be a 'thespian' and was planning to go first to community college and then a local university to major in theatre. It may be that theatre—as a field with university majors and, therefore, greater visibility— was less emblematic of newer occupations in the creative industries. Unlike the other narratives, when asked why she spent time at Young Creatives and not somewhere else, Tonya told a story with a clear relationship between Young Creatives, college, and her future career in the arts:

> I felt that Young Creatives gives me a chance to grow in something that I actually do want to make a career out of when I get out of college and when I step into a studio like Sigma Sound, then I will have not only the degree to back me up but the experience that Young Creatives has given me.
>
> (Peer interview)

Other interviewees spoke about their goals to make it in various fields. Their strategies were focused on talent development and network development, rather than through a sequence of institutional credentials. Courtney said that after college, she planned to get 'a little bit farther into the music business than I already am. Probably meeting people, making beats for them. Just getting to know them professionally so I can slowly ease my way into the music business.' Meeting people and continuing to produce music were steps Courtney understood as part of the process of finding work. Nearly all peers indicated that attending college was their planned next step, but unlike the STEM Mentoring students, most of these respondents did not draw explicit connections between their artistic interests and their field of study in college.

Strategies to Build Pathways in Creative Industries

STEM Mentoring functioned in a way that was suited to the specific barriers in the STEM ecosystem; it offered free high-quality training that could give young people with limited financial resources access to and credentials to succeed along a competitive STEM pathway. What about strategies for programmes facing the more opaque, precarious field of new media arts? We observed two strategies: building an internal pathway and catalysing entrepreneurship.

Building a Stable Local Pathway

Young Creatives created entrepreneurial ventures that employed youth in digital arts activities. For example, Jonny, a programme teacher and mentor, described 'Young Creatives Industries':

> Young Creatives Industries is separate from my animation and photography class. Young Creatives Industries—we're actually starting a photography business. They started it. They're off and running. Right now, we're building a web site because you want to start advertising for their event photography, for the photo booth, and for portrait photography. We're in the process of building a web site that showcases their strengths and their work and what they've done so far, so we can go out and advertise and bring in clients and start getting their name out.
>
> (Mentor interview)

Jonny's story shows a key strategy employed by Young Creatives to support students' progress along the new media arts pathway: *build it*. Kathy, who was one of Young Creatives Industries students, explained the value of building a website and learning more about photography: 'Sooner or later, we're going to have real jobs, so we're getting prepared for it.' Young Creatives Industries provided clarity about the creative ecosystem by creating opportunities for students to not simply practice or simulate relevant skills but instead actually generate revenue through their projects and expertise.

Opportunities like Young Creatives Industries were accompanied by multiple stories of participants or alumni who had been hired to help teach, mentor, or lead programmes in Young Creatives as they got older. Jeff described how he 'never left' Young Creatives, because, even after his time as a student, he 'still used to come through, help out with classes, help video students.' Jeff worked on the landscaping crew but had also recently been invited to become the videography teacher. Jennifer, a mentor, also made note of other alumni who had returned to Young Creatives. For her, making job opportunities available was tied to maintaining ties to youth and cultivating their sense of community support.

> Then giving students jobs [. . .]. That's a way to keep them coming back of course. Knowing that we ultimately, I think this organization,

Young Creatives, looks out for kids. As soon as you come here, you've got a whole family of people that are looking out for you as much as you'll allow them to.

(Mentor interview)

A success story referenced by multiple interviewees centred on a current staff member who achieved wider recognition after developing his skills in Young Creatives.

Jeff came here as a little kid, and then he went through the program. Then he came back, and now he's making videos with A. Now he has a very successful video that he's made that they've gotten into all sorts of film festivals all over the country. Now he's teaching here. I feel like he's a very strong mentor. He's also doing all kinds of stuff in the art world and the video on his own and without.

(Mentor interview)

This notion of building pathways and creating employment opportunities within the organisation is something that has been observed in other programmes focused on new media arts (e.g. O'Connor & Allen, 2010; Soep & Chávez, 2010).

Entrepreneurship

In addition to providing opportunities for paid employment through Young Creatives Industries, Young Creatives also celebrated and encouraged participants in its programmes to strike out on their own as entrepreneurs. This emphasis on entrepreneurship was a sign of how in creative industries, experience, networks, and talent hold more weight than credentials or formal education. Jeff spoke about a programme for people returning from incarceration, which teaches video production and editing. He said, 'That way, they can open their own selves up for job opportunities, and they don't have to depend on other people to make money. And they can just go ahead, and go chase a couple dollars themselves.' Jeff went on to talk about this effort by Young Creatives to respond to people's need for income and to provide support for their own entrepreneurship:

Everything is about getting to a dollar now. . . . We're going to teach you this, that way if you ever need a job, you can say . . . 'Okay, I've got years in doing such and such. I've got years of schooling at engineering or beat making or video,' anything of that nature. . . . Everything here right now is based upon getting to a dollar and finding a career that suits you, that you will love.

(Alumni interview)

Jeff's comments, echoing Kim's take that 'you can find jobs anywhere,' reflected a tendency to put stock in the capacity of talented youth to use their training and skill development for success in creative industries. We did not hear of examples of active or intentional brokering to these external opportunities by Young Creatives staff, but instead a general belief that Young Creatives offered the space to develop skills and talent that then would be leveraged for further work.

Conclusion

Programme features emphasised in positive youth development (PYD) literature, such as sense of belonging and opportunities for skill development, were abundant in both STEM Mentoring and Young Creatives. These core areas of focus for PYD, however, although providing valuable guidance for the design of programmes, leave programmes unequipped to conceptualise or design for transitions to sustainable livelihoods as people age out of youth programmes. As shown in our data, young people's narratives about pathways into fields of STEM and creative arts differed when it came to seeking opportunities beyond their respective programmes. It is true that there may be other explanations for the different narratives, including the slightly different demographics of the two programmes and their locations in different cities. But we think these examples are suggestive of meaningful differences, linked to distinct fields, which call for further attention from researchers and practitioners.

These differences, for example, point to the importance of closer examination of the telos of various programmes and how this telos is supported or not in a broader ecosystem (Penuel, Clark, & Bevan, 2016). Young people's trajectories are shaped by the visibility, institutional recognition, and relative openness of the social future for which they are preparing. These dimensions of visibility and openness helped to describe nuanced differences in fields and the ways in which youth programmes support young people to navigate them. This is particularly salient when it comes to the emerging field of digital media arts. As we discussed in the introduction to this volume, programmes in digital media arts may need to place greater emphasis on building or organising pathways for youth—and making those pathways more recognisable and consequential—in order to help youth pursue and sustain their interests in a field that tends to be less stable, more opaque, and more open: see also Chapter 5. In this sense, the emphasis on career *readiness*, so common in the rhetoric of US policymakers, is misplaced without parallel attention to readying a stronger web of networks and opportunities for creatively inclined youth. This would mean that the work of youth programmes is taken up not only with mentoring youth or teaching them skills but also organising institutions and people to create networked opportunities for young creatives.

Such a shift calls for more expansive definitions of programme quality and what it means to support youths' access to careers in the arts.

Notes

1. Mature participation is a term from sociocultural learning theory referring to the end point of development and exemplified by the roles and practices played by 'old-hands' in a social community (Rogoff, 2003).
2. The Connected Learning Research Network (CLRN), with funding from the MacArthur Foundation, was a network of scholars exploring questions related to connected learning in the digital age (see Ito et al., 2013). A sub-study within the CLRN, led by Kirshner, invited young people to work as co-researchers studying aspects of their learning experiences.

References

Barron, B. (2004). Learning ecologies for technological fluency: Gender and experience differences. *Journal of Educational Computing Research*, *31*(1), 1–36.

Barron, B. (2006). Interest and self-sustained learning as catalysts of development: A learning ecologies perspective. *Human Development*, *49*, 193–224.

Barron, B., Gomez, K., Pinkard, N., Martin, C. K., Austin, K., Gray, T. . . . Zywica, J. (2014). *The digital youth network: Cultivating digital media citizenship in urban communities*. Cambridge, MA: MIT Press.

Barron, B., Wise, S., & Martin, C. K. (2012). Creating within and across life spaces: The role of a computer clubhouse in a child's learning ecology. In B. Bevan, P. Bell, R. Stevens, & A. Razfar (Eds.), *Lost opportunities: Explorations of educational purpose* (Vol. 23, pp. 99–118). Dordrecht, Netherlands: Springer.

Bourdieu, P. (1998). *On television and journalism*. London, UK: Pluto Press.

Brown, J. S., Collins, A., & Duguid, P. (1989). Situated cognition and the culture of learning. *Education Researcher*, *18*(1), 32–42.

Ching, D., Santo, R., Hoadley, C., & Peppler, K. (2015). *On-ramps, lane changes, detours and destinations: Building connected learning pathways in Hive NYC through brokering future learning opportunities*. New York, NY: Hive Research Lab.

Deschenes, S., Little, P., Grossman, J., & Arbreton, A. (2010). Participation over time: Keeping youth engaged from middle school to high school. *Afterschool Matters*, 1–8.

Gomez, K., Barron, B., & Pinkard, N. (2014). Introduction: The digital media landscape. In B. Barron, K. Gomez, N. Pinkard, C. K. Martin, K. Austin, T. Gray . . . J. Zywica (Eds.), *The digital youth network: Cultivating digital media citizenship in urban communities* (pp. 1–13). Cambridge, MA: MIT Press.

Gutiérrez, K. D. (2008). Developing a sociocritical literacy in the third space. *Reading Research Quarterly*, *43*(2), 148–164.

Gutiérrez, K. D., Cortes, K., Cortez, A., DiGiacomo, D., Higgs, J., Johnson, P., . . . Vakil, S. (2017). Replacing representation with imagination: Finding ingenuity in everyday practices. *Review of Research in Education*, *41*(1), 30–60. https://doi.org/10.3102/0091732X16687523

Gutiérrez, K. D., Morales, P. Z., & Martinez, D. C. (2009). Re-mediating literacy: Culture, difference, and learning for students from nondominant communities. *Review of Research in Education, 33,* 212–245.

Hall, R., & Jurow, A. S. (2015). Changing concepts in activity: Descriptive and design studies of consequential learning across time, space, and social organization. *Educational Psychologist, 50*(3), 173–189.

Herr-Stephenson, B., Rhoten, D., Perkel, D., & Sims, C. (2011). *Digital media and technology in afterschool programs, libraries, and museums.* Cambridge, MA: MIT Press. Retrieved from http://mitpress.mit.edu/books/full_pdfs/Digital_Media_and_Technology_in_Afterschool_Programs.pdf

Hull, G. A., & Katz, M.-L. (2006). Crafting an agentive self: Case studies of digital storytelling. *Research in the Teaching of English, 41*(1), 43–81.

Ito, M., Guitiérrez, K., Livingstone, S., Penuel, B., Rhodes, J., Salen, K., Schor, J., Sefton-Green, J., Watkins, C. S. (2013). *Connected learning: An agenda for research and design.* Irvine, CA: Digital Media and Learning Research Hub. Retrieved from http://dmlhub.net/publications/connected-learning-agenda-research-and-design

Jurow, S., Horn, I. S., & Philip, T. M. (2018). Re-mediating knowledge infrastructures: A site for innovation in teacher education. *Journal of Education for Teaching, 45*(1), 1–15. https://doi.org/10.1080/02607476.2019.1550607

Lave, J. (1996). The practice of learning. In S. Chaiklin & J. Lave (Eds.), *Understanding practice: Perspectives on activity and context* (pp. 3–34). Cambridge, UK: Cambridge University Press.

Lee, D. (2011). Networks, cultural capital and creative labour in the British independent television industry. *Media, Culture & Society, 33*(4), 549–565.

Lingard, B., & Christie, P. (2003). Leading theory: Bourdieu and the field of educational leadership. An introduction and overview to this special issue. *International Journal of Leadership in Education, 6*(4), 317–333. https://doi.org/10.1080/1360312032000150724

McLaughlin, M. W. (2000). *Community counts: How youth organizations matter for youth development.* Washington, DC: Public Education Network.

National Research Council. (2002). *Community programs to promote youth development.* Washington, DC: National Academies Press.

Neff, G., Wissinger, E., & Zukin, S. (2005). Entrepreneurial labor among cultural producers: "Cool" jobs in "hot" industries. *Social Semiotics, 15*(3), 307–334. https://doi.org/10.1080/10350330500310111

New London Group. (1996). A pedagogy of multiliteracies: Designing social futures. *Harvard Educational Review, 66*(1), 309–327.

O'Connor, K., & Allen, A.-R. (2010). Learning as the organizing of social futures. *NSSE Yearbook, 109*(1), 160–175.

Penuel, W. R., Clark, T. L., & Bevan, B. (2016). Infrastructures to support equitable STEM learning across settings. *Afterschool Matters,* Fall(24), 12–20.

Penuel, W. P., & O'Connor, K. (2010). Learning research as a human science: Old wine in new bottles? *Yearbook of the National Society for the Study of Education, 109*(1), 268–283.

Richards, K. A., Gomez, K., & Gray, T. (2014). iRemix education: Engaging mentors as teachers. In The Digital Youth Network (Eds.), *The digital youth network: Cultivating digital media citizenship in urban communities* (pp. 48–72). Cambridge, MA: MIT Press.

Rogoff, B. (2003). *The cultural nature of human development.* New York, NY: Oxford University Press.

Sawyer, R. K. (Ed.). (2005). *The Cambridge handbook of the learning sciences.* Cambridge, UK: Cambridge University Press.

Sefton-Green, J., & Brown, L. (2014). *Mapping learner progression into digital creativity: Catalysts & disconnects.* Nominet Trust State of the Art Reviews. Retrieved from https://socialtechtrust.org/wp-content/uploads/2017/11/Mapping-learner-progression-into-digital-creativity-FINAL.pdf

Soep, E., & Chávez, V. (2010). *Drop that knowledge: Youth radio stories.* Berkeley, CA: University of California Press.

Strobel, K., Kirshner, B., McLaughlin, M. W., & O'Donoghue, J. (2008). Qualities that attract urban youth to after-school settings and promote continued participation. *Teachers College Record, 110*(8), 1677–1705.

Van Steenis, E., & Kirshner, B. (in press). Hip-hop music making as a context for relational equity among youth and youth workers. In Brion-Meisels, G., Vasudevan, D., & Fee, J. (Eds.), *Authentic partnerships between adults and youth in out-of-school time* settings. Charlotte, NC: Information Age Press.

Varenne, H., & McDermott, R. (1999). *Successful failure: The school America builds.* Boulder, CO: Westview Press.

Warde, A. (2004). *Practice and field: Revising Bourdieusian concepts.* CRIC Discussion Paper No 65. Manchester, UK: The University of Manchester. Retrieved from www.researchgate.net/publication/238096928_Practice_and_Field_Revising_Bourdieusian_Concepts

York, A. (2015). *Guided participation in creative civic practices.* Boulder, CO: University of Colorado.

Zeller-Berkman, S. (2010). Critical development? Using a critical theory lens to examine the current role of evaluation in the youth-development field. *New Directions for Evaluation, 127*, 35–44. https://doi.org/10.1002/ev.337

Index

Note: page numbers in *italics* indicate figures; page numbers in **bold** indicate tables.

For Product Safety Concerns and Information please contact our EU
representative GPSR@taylorandfrancis.com
Taylor & Francis Verlag GmbH, Kaufingerstraße 24, 80331 München, Germany